Cooling Time

Also by C.D. Wright

C.D. WRIGHT

Cooling Time

An American Poetry Vigil

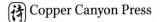 Copper Canyon Press

Cover art: *Man/Beast,* by Douglas Humble. Interior art also by Douglas Humble.

Copper Canyon Press is in residence at Fort Worden State Park in Port Townsend, Washington, under the auspices of Centrum Foundation. Centrum is a gathering place for artists and creative thinkers from around the world, students of all ages and backgrounds, and audiences seeking extraordinary cultural enrichment.

LIBRARY OF CONGRESS CATALOGING-IN-PUBLICATION DATA
Wright, C.D., 1949–
Cooling time: an American poetry vigil / C.D. Wright.
  p. cm.
ISBN 1-55659-216-7 (pbk.: alk. paper)
1. Poetry — Authorship.   2. Poetry.   I. Title.
PS3573.R497C66 2004
811'.54 — DC22

2004010115

9 8 7 6 5 4 3 2
FIRST PRINTING

COPPER CANYON PRESS
Post Office Box 271
Port Townsend, Washington 98368
www.coppercanyonpress.org

for Forrest and for Brecht
who live with this contrarian

ACKNOWLEDGMENTS

This work describes a selection of passages taken from various of my talks, essays, articles, and interviews. I would like to thank the editors and publishers of the journals, anthologies, and books from which these passages were excerpted: *Antioch Review; Arkansas Times; BRICK; By Herself; Caliban; Conjunctions; Chronicle of the Associated Writing Programs; Cross Roads: Journal of the Poetry Society of America; Field; Five Fingers Review; Further Adventures with You; George Street Journal; The Grand Permission: New Writing on Poetics and Motherhood; Helicon 9; Hungry Mind Review; Ironwood; Jacket; Jubilat; Kenyon Review; Language Change: Poetry, Politics and Common Usage; Onward: Contemporary Poetry and Poetics;* PEN *America; Ploughshares; Poetry East; Poetry Pilot; Poetry Speaks; Providence Journal Sunday Magazine; raccoon; Quarter After Eight; The Southern Review; String Light; Teachers & Writers.* I further wish to thank the following institutions and organizations for inviting the talks or papers from which some of these selections were made: the Associated Writing Programs, Breadloaf Writers Conference, Brown University, Carleton College, Cranbrook Academy of Art, Intersection Center for the Arts, The Light Factory, Lyon College, Mary Ingraham Bunting Institute at Radcliffe College, Poetry Society of America, University at Buffalo Anderson Gallery, University of Central Arkansas, University of Louisville. The poems "in our only time." and "until words turn to moss." were first published in *NO*, #1, winter 2003. "only the crossing counts." was published first in *sulfur*, spring 2000. "elation washed over our absence toward everything in the increasing darkness." in *Slate*, winter 1999.

The author thanks the editors and staff of Copper Canyon Press, whose participation is always good-spirited, copious, and professional. Especial thanks to David Caligiuri.

I would also like to thank the Lannan Foundation for a 1999 Literary Award and for a month-long residency in Marfa, Texas, in the summer of 2003, which facilitated the completion of this work.

Please note that every attempt has been made to quote and attribute accurately, though my cacography is pure D hell to decipher.

Cooling Time: a line of legal defense, peculiar to Texas courts, in which it is held that if a man kills before he has had time "to cool" after receiving an injury or an insult he is not guilty of murder. (Footnoted in William Humphrey's 1965 novel, *The Ordways.*)

No one expects ballplayers to comprehend the implications of their work.

RON SILLIMAN

The time has come to loot to hew and Eden.

MARJORIE MILLIGAN

Cooling Time

Op-Ed

I believe in a hardheaded art, an unremitting, unrepentant practice of one's own faith in the word in one's own obstinate terms. I believe the word was made good from the start; it remains so to this second. I believe words are golden as goodness is golden. Even the humble word *brush* gives off a scratch of light. There is not much poetry from which I feel barred, whether it is arcane or open in the extreme. I attempt to run the gamut because I am pulled by the extremes. I believe the word used wrongly distorts the world. I hold to hard distinctions of right and wrong. Also I think that antithetical poetries can and should coexist without crippling one another. They not only serve to define their other to a much more exacting degree than would be possible in the absence of the one or the other; they insure the persistence of heterogeneous (albeit discouragingly small) constituencies. While I am not always equal to it, I appreciate the fray. I am neither too old for it nor too finished off. I am not sure of where it is I am going. Important, I believe, to resist finality in one's own work while assiduously working toward its completeness. Detrimental, I think, the dread of being passed on the left, as is the deluded and furthermore trivializing notion of one's own work being an advance over any thing or any one. Truthfulness is crucial. A continuous self-criticism is demanded of the effort without which only non-art gets made, that is, manufactured. "A poet would show little thought to say poetry is opposed to since it is added to like science," insisted Zukofsky. So do I, insist. Consequently I would contest those writers whose end is (reviling-all-the-way) to prevail.

Provisionally yours,

Every year the poem I most want to write, the poem that would in effect allow me to stop writing, changes shapes, changes directions. It refuses to come forward, to stand still while I move to meet it, embrace and coax it to sit on the porch with me and watch the lightning bugs steal behind the fog's heavy veil, listen for the drag of johnboats through the orchestra of locusts and frogs. An old handplow supports the mailbox, a split-rail fence borders the front lot. Hollyhocks and sunflowers loom there. At the end of the lot the road forks off to the left toward the river, to the right toward the old chicken slaughterhouse. The poem hangs back, wraithlike, yet impenetrable as briar. The porch is more impressive than the rest of the house. A moth as big as a girl's hand spreads itself out on the screendoor. The house smells like beets. For in this poem it is always Arkansas, summer, evening. But in truth, the poem never sleeps unless I do, for if I were to come upon it sleeping, I would net it. And that would be that, my splendid catch.

In my book poetry is a necessity of life, what they used to call nontaxable matter. I cannot objectively trace how I reached this exaggerated conclusion, but perhaps I can summon the origins for my brand of tectonics in what would seem to many to be an age antithetical to the effort. Ultimately I don't believe any age is antithetical to the effort. I do believe years of reaction promote a thwarted artistic front. "Art is like ham," Diego Rivera said. I have often been reassured by this inexplicable claim. "Sometimes art (poetry) is like a beautiful sick dog that shits all over the house," Frank Stanford scribbled in a notebook. Not without a twinge of sadness, I agree with this claim too.

Many writers maintain a guarded border between language thick with hair and twigs and the reified, rarified stuff. No matter which side of the border poets live on, they tend to act as if they were being overrun. All I want is a day pass. I like to sleep in my own bed.

My purpose is neither to hack away at the canon nor to contrive a trend.

I am interested in fertile poetic constructions. I am aiming for the ode as a recourse, however short-term, from the same-old same-old careerist poem of no note, no risk, and no satisfaction, and from the equally piggish obsession with newness. The search for models in my terms becomes a search for alternatives.

My whole life I thought I was meant to do something useful — not for everyone, nothing on the scale of inventing Kleenex and making a pile for doing it, but something in which I felt the usefulness of it, the goodness of it in a non-Byzantine* way. And I have come to feel separated from the possibility of being useful because I am an American poet. Maybe I did not choose poetry primarily because I believed it to be a necessary good, but I have abided by it because I believe this. Unlike, say, Oppen, I am not a purist. I am capable and comfortable with many vulgarities both in word and deed, especially in word. And I did not understand when I made this commitment that

*Byzantine, Byzantinism, or Scholasticism employs here Gramsci's usage, meaning the regressive tendency to treat so-called theoretical questions as if they had a value in themselves, independently of any practice — a principle put forth in the *Prison Notebooks.*

to choose being a poet meant I would be speaking what David Antin refers to as "a sacred language... the object of a specialized cult." Or if I did have such an inkling when I first undertook to write poetry, I didn't think anything was wrong with that at the time. Now I am sure poetry's lot is as he defined it and I oppose this exclusive and near meaningless status, yet I persist. Therefore, some quasi-futile, sometimes productive, psychic suffering.

Never put yourself in the position of having to defend the work before it is done.

Poetry is like food, remarked one of my first teachers, freeing me to dislike Rocky Mountain oysters and Robert Lowell. The menu is vast, the list of things I don't want in my mouth relatively short.

I am looking for a way to vocalize, perform, act out, address the commonly felt crises of my time. These are spiritual exercises.

Verbal energy on my part is expended on packing words down. I am concerned with density, setting up a chain reaction using the least amount of verbal material.

Much has been declared about the musicality of poetry. Not so much about the physicality. The adamantine practice of poetry as it pertains to touch — an impression of which can be lifted off the ends of the fingers. These are some of the things I have touched in my life that are forbidden: paintings behind velvet ropes, electric fencing, a vault in an office, gun in a drawer, my brother's folding money, the poet's anus, the black holes in his heart — where his life went out of him.

Phrases I prefer to associate with the lexicon of music rather than of linguistics, that is, the distinctiveness of a poetic phrase seems better identified among notes, tones, and rhythms, than among word aggregates with a single stress. By which I intend to say, a phrase is a sensory unit, physical but furthermore felt, not simply syntactic. *A cold rain.* is a phrase to me. And a sentence. So is what follows the rain, *Quiet as a mirror.* As are: *A praying mantis in a jar. Barns blown down. Her rainy underarms. Faith hope and hypocrisy,* phrases and sentences. Near physical beings to my way of sounding/thinking/feeling. I tune my instrument against my own eardrums.

Tell me, what is the long stretch of road for if not to sort out the reasons why we are here and why we do what we do, from why we are not in the other lane doing what others do.

We come from a country that has made a fetish if not a virtue out of proving it can live without art: high, low, old, new, fat, lean, and particularly the rarely visible, nocturnal art of poetry.

We must do something with our time on this small aleatory sphere for motives other than money. Power is not an acceptable surrogate.*

I am even willing to argue passion is what separates us from other life-forms — that is, beyond the power to reason is our ability to escape from the desert of pure reason by its own primary instrument, language. And if it be poetry that makes the words flesh, then it is no less or more escapable than our bodies. But it is at least that free.

Veering in the elusory direction of freedom, I would submit, it is a function of poetry to locate those zones inside us that would be free and declare them so. Always there are restrictions: as traditional conventions are more or less disavowed, others remain constant for longer periods, and another is revived after long periods of disuse. Poetry without form is a fiction. But that there is a freedom in words is the larger fact, and in poetry, where formal restrictions can bear down heavily, it is important to remember the cage is never locked.

I have been a keen but unsystematic student of book-length poems, in substance and design. Length admits them to the novel's province of inclusivity and digression, but redoubles the requisite for form. The need for form arises not so much for containment but for support. Form naturally determines the poem's movement, whether it be gradual, teleological, furious, or traveling in reverse. Otherwise, the stasis of art prose. Ugh.

*The eclectic Bulgarian scholar Elias Canetti fastidiously stylized his 550-page study *Crowds and Power* to conclude simply, "To be the last man to remain alive is the deepest urge of every real seeker after power."

At the margins of poetry, form is forced out of the frame under
the sheer pressure of the language.

Five of us hold down the lines at The Poetry Center. Two in the
archives. Three in the main office. We organize talks and read-
ings, then videotape and distribute these events on a lending
basis. For the students we also provide audiotapes, three
bookcases, and a nondescript sofa. Some are regulars: D.F.
Brown, a Vietnam veteran, poet, native of Springfield; Forrest
Gander, a Virginia poet, formerly a student of geology. Brown
discovered poetry, rather was discovered by poetry, when he
was nineteen and a half, in the infantry. Binh Dinh province.
He was a nurse. In the infantry. A man of nineteen and a half.
Boxes of books came to the base camp. For one reason or
another Brown was habitually slow in reaching the mailroom,
the last to rifle the book boxes, poetry the last to be rifled.
After everything else, all the serious literature, all the theology,
all the pulp and the porn, poetry would remain. On bottom,
undisturbed. With little choice and less enthusiasm, Brown
picked up a work by Robert Creeley. Thus one more of us was
born: as gravity came to Newton and enlightenment to
Siddhārtha.

With a Creeley line, the mind doesn't need to fill in every word
as it natters to itself; we know what he means, what he is
thinking, what he sees. We've been invited. Inside. And if he
chooses to interrupt himself, to pause abruptly, to leave a
sentence uncompleted — we know what he means, what he is
thinking, what he sees. We've been invited. He gives the gist.
We are his familiars, the lines suggest. He can skip; he allows
himself, and us, breathing room, and he is so unassuming in

his friendliness that we permit his regulation of our very breath with big space, "unnatural" breaks, a poetic notation of his own devising. A line of three syllables much more frequent than one of twelve. A margin on the left as wide as the one on the right. A jarring break, as if stepping off a curb one didn't see, but catching and righting oneself midair. Perhaps there is something to the single eye informing the line; as El Greco's shapes were likely derived in part from an alleged astigmatism, Creeley's partial-sightedness intensifies attention to the center, drafting the outside, inside. The focus hangs in the middle, where emotion-bearing thought drops its plumb bob.

Poetry is tribal not material. As such it lights the fire and keeps watch over the flame. Believe me, this is where you get warm again. And naked. This is where you can remember the good times along with the worst; where you are not allowed to forget the worst, else you cannot be healed. This is where your memory must be exacting — where you and your progeny are held accountable but also laudable. Even and especially in our day, in our amnesiac land, poets are the griots, the ones who see that the word does not break faith with the line of the body.

I believe that many members of "the tribe" — not to say that we were the first but that we were the last — suffer the retrenchment of human possibilities, possibilities which for our thousand-and-one errors, we helped to create, which include the right and the delight in choosing writing, even writing poetry, over lawyering, banking, spying, advertising, politicking, and other predatory arts, and that in helping to create these possibilities we simultaneously infected other areas of the population with similar yearnings. Of course we failed, and of course it was doomed given the country's whole direction post–World War II, given our whole carnal history — after all, we called ourselves having a democracy *in situ* when we were the only remaining country publicly auctioning off our own species. Nevertheless, the tribe has some right to pride in our resistance, and to be pained by the losses that include, not bottom on my list, the further devaluation of poetry. "What lays waste my heart / lays waste, lays waste my art," Sharon Doubiago wrote in her big, declarative poem of America, *Hard Country*.

The bottom dropping out of a sack of black apples is dramatic enough for what I want to tell, which is after all proposed, not actual. If I tried too hard to be revelatory, well that was then. I don't try that hard now. I know life is strange and reveals itself on its own terms. The word is all that is the case. Now: a man joins a woman in the kitchen. They touch the soft places of their fruit. They enter in, tell their side, and pass through.

Forrest Gander would graduate from San Francisco State that spring. Gravely personal circumstances had brought him to poetry also. Concentrating both in earth science and English as an undergraduate at William and Mary, smitten by melanoma, spared but chastened, he chose poetry over, let's face it, a gig with an oil company hunting for uranium deposits. Not for the lodestone. Not for the locus Beckett plats for us, "...already old. The ditch is old. In the beginning it was all bright. All bright dots. It does not encroach on the dark. Adamantine darkness of these. As dense at the edge as at the centre..." It would not be in Texaco's interest to locate any position so remote and near as what Beckett described, which could be an acre of hell on earth. Or heaven. The dually maintained residences of poetry.

The Box This Comes In

is not beautiful, at least it is not aggressively beautiful, meaning the workmanship, as it was formerly called — regardless who took up the tools, but also generally reflecting to whom the tools were entrusted — falls on the faulty side, connoting the work shows: nail heads, cuts that exceeded their mark in ensuring the fit of the lid, steel screws securing brass hinges, and especially the irregular tooling of the conventionalized flowers. Though the flowers are suggestive of tulips and dogwood they are apt to be fleurs-de-lis and marvels-of-Peru. Because the work shows, I favor it more. It likewise follows, lacking mechanical perfection, the box was made by hand — possibly for someone in particular rather than for sale. If the object were wages not affection, it was nevertheless made with the same two hands. Practice rather than mastery guided its making. If true to tradition, the maker's profit would have been unduly low. For motives ruled by affection the making would have been its own reward. The box was given to me by an old flame, now a virtually unbeaten trial lawyer. And we were ourselves oft bound by a kind of consummate argument. In the end I was the wounded, but throughout I inflicted my rude, overbearing manner on him. Memories too keen to dwell upon.

The first woman it was made or bought for has long occupied her own box. So does the maker — occupy a box of his own, that is if we follow the gender assumptions of the period in which it was made — by him, for her. On the other hand, the flowers are on the austere side, not overly feminine; perhaps it was meant to hold a man's effects. There is no loitering odor of cigars or of perfume. The wood is dark. The lining vanished but for the residual glue-tracks and morsels of fabric attesting it was once faced with gold velvet. It measures 6⅞ × 11 inches.

The interior space offers an inch less in length and width, again to ensure the lid's fit. The box stands 3 inches tall.

Allow me to date it this way: the woman, whom I won't try to picture in detail, must have had a bundle of hair, as when it was bought for me fifteen years ago; the dealer told my friend it was approximately sixty years old. Circa 1914. This would have been prior to the bob, a coif forbidden to this day according to an Arkansas statute. Little Rock is where it was bought but not where it necessarily originated. The antique dealers in that internal capital get around to wherever dealers in old things convene, and they venture out on their own: estate sales, flea markets, bank auctions. A dreamy novel could be written about the alleged maker and the alleged recipient, but merely to dream them up in period clothing, in love and trouble, does not stir me. I am more drawn to cold, factual things such as diet, income, fertility, abilities with animals, plants, interstellar links.

If I knew my woods once felled and fashioned, I would tell you what wood this is, what polish to apply. Generically, my guess is fruitwood, if this does not infer too gorgeous a grain. Of trees in leaf or bloom, I am on a first-name basis with an impressive number, even the paulownia, resembling the catalpa, which, alongside the mimosa, is treated as a nuisance tree in the little towns in the mountains as their frilly flowers damage car finish. Where cars are inviolable, totemic. The bodark remains my personal favorite — it being truly hard, burning blue in the fireplace and standing out by itself in a field with its extra half-dozen monikers: hedge apple, horse apple, mock orange, Osage orange, bow wood, bois d'arc, not to mention its bizarre globular fruit and lascivious smell.

Diagonally across the lid stretches an ugly scar, unprofessionally repaired. The result of some lapse. Even from the underside the injury appears in reverse. The flowers that lace the lid and sides have been tipped with gold paint. One hopes that the painter did not wet the brushes with the inside of the mouth to bring them to a fine point in order to articulate the scrolling stems, because the odds are, the pigment is tainted with a pretty poison.

The box holds a trifling inventory of things kept in spite of their inverse relation to value: Two bow ties, one solid avocado green but patterned, one with lavender and pink diamonds on a purplish field (from my father's springy days). Three battery-operated watches, a strand of phony pearls, six or seven non-descript drugstore barrettes, one Italian butterfly clasp (for my sheared head). Clay beads from the Chrysler Museum shop in Norfolk (because they were a dollar and because I was burning to buy something). Three flowered handkerchiefs from Mamo, carefully folded inside her last birthday card to me—of the type she carried in her handbag since she was a young woman to blot the lips, tamp the brow, blow the nose (although I can't for the life of me see myself blotting, tamping, much less blowing on them). One has been folded so as to bloom from a breast pocket. A black ribbon for an armband when the occasion calls (last donned Election Day, 1980). A strip of Day-Glo surveyor's tape pierced by an ordinary nail that belonged to Frank Stanford, poet, land surveyor. According to the late Stanford, the tape derives from a vegetable base; cows love it, causing the line just surveyed and flagged to vanish behind you. Also, one notably odd handkerchief brought back for a souvenir of Seoul: short parallel pink and aqua bars on a white cotton field surrounding a square frame that features a pig in a zoot suit. The pig stands in front of a tractor parked before a limelighted city. A poem inscribes the picture: "Listen, Can you hear the Manhattan blues? / Howdi? / Smoky Night. Moody shadow is behind my back. Slow ballad / is in my glass. Black trick is a sweet thing. City light is only my god." My notion of Seoul nights is undoubtedly as accurate as the Korean poet's of Manhattan's. One fabric gardenia, misshapen and discolored.

One lacquered poppy from the Legionnaires. Three woven friendship bracelets, a pewter and enamel cross once on a poet's key chain. A silver dollar from Mamo, tin dragonfly from Jean Kondo, a malachite necklace, unstrung, two frosted hair combs bought in a jewelry store in a small-town mall on the eve of my wedding. One star-shaped turquoise pin, one beaded, leather ring I cannot remember borrowing or buying, neither of which I like even a little.

The box maintains an honored place on my sewing machine bought at the sewing center on Broad Street because it is there, which is near, and because I imagined myself sewing, curved over yards of washable silk, giving the balance wheel a spin and treadling until the dress was done. Then I would put it on and go where, to the policeman's ball? "Howdi, Smoky Night." On my rickety Mamo's one-and-only visit to Rhode Island she showed me how to thread my Singer. I did not progress beyond threading nor did Mamo's recollection extend to stitching. The only one in my immediate family who can minimally claim current use of a sewing machine is my father, retired jurist, who bought a White at a yard sale. Actually Judge persuaded my mother to make the purchase for him while he sat in the car feigning manly disinterest. The cemeteries are rife with people who knew how to make them hum. The Singer mechanism itself has been retired to the attic. Over the well, I placed a jagged slab of veined green marble fallen off the front of a building downtown. On top of the slab a covered glazed bowl from the kilns of Gubbio — where we waited out a sudden, fabulous storm before a long, fabulous supper. The bowl I filled with cotton balls. Also on the marble, an array of shapely jars and bottles of clarifying lotion, moisturizer, emollient, eau de toilette. Propped against the wall behind them, a tin mirror from Mexico. I perform my ablutions there. Of a morning and an evening, I face myself, a poet of forty. Within the limits of this diminutive wooden world, I have made do with the cracks of light and tokens of loss and recovery that came my way. I can offer no more explicit demonstration as to what my poetry is. The box this comes in is mine;

I remain faithfully,

I have never thought it hyperbole to say coming to poetry is a near-death experience. I myself arrived here after a succession of losses. Lastly, after the death by suicide of Frank Stanford, poet from Arkansas. I inherited his small debts, Lost Roads Publishers, the book press he started, half the gorgeous corpus of his work (the adamantine darkness of these), his devotion to the crooked, humpbacked letters that make up Mississippi, and the rest of that legendary water's burdensome tongue.

The one poetry broadside in the lounge at my college read, *Practice practice put your faith in that,* signed W.S. Merwin. After the building was painted, it no longer hung there and I felt my resolve weaken.

Synchronous with so much deliberation, an element of spontaneity must be exacted. To draft us into the situation, the situation should be ongoing. However, it should not be inclusive, not try to show beginning, middle, and end.

Closure can be avoided by as many strategies as can beginning. "Endings just drag me," Miles Davis said in a *Down Beat* interview.

One configuration I admire is distichous. Symmetrical asymmetry. Clarity pressed into opacity. One sentence allowing the one behind it to pass.

Forrest Gander took his first out-of-college job at the methadone clinic in downtown San Francisco. Something to do with forms. I would hold down the lines at The Poetry Center a few months longer, filling out papers in quadruplicate for the campus foundation through which every penny awarded our shoestring outfit had to pass and forfeit a percentage. After work, Forrest and I would meet for a movie or stir-fried. Or I would go to the women's gym and he would go home to write or go to the Japanese cinema. We lived nearby then, but not together.

While lyric is traditionally viewed as being at the opposite end of narration, it seems a drastically inept and unfulfilling term for the kinds of machines now feeding onto the expressway. The term *lyric* — though it might suggest a larger area of abstraction than does *narrative* — satisfies but a portion of poems being written in real contrast to recognizable narratives.

An atmosphere of depression will arouse artists' attention over an atmosphere of prosperity nearly every time. Also true, ruins are beautiful to us; blues make us feel good; it is through the wound that we perceive the body alive alive-o.

Hopefully, we have come a long way from currying the favor of royalty — from the original laureates. We have returned to our more enduring function as seers. Naturally some see better and farther than others.

For we cometh, for we cometh to judge the light paling the door, not the dark halls it obscures.

My San Francisco roommate was an archivist at The Poetry Center. And an archivist at home where he collected music, books, magazines. A redheaded fiction writer from Oklahoma. On a visit back to Bartlesville he had taped an electrical storm; when he needed to renew himself he wriggled into his sleeping bag in our dingy apartment on Potrero Hill and listened to the lightning crack through the loudspeakers. I went to the only bar on the hill, played "Wild Horses" on the jukebox, did my laundry or thought about doing laundry, ate a burrito or a stale piroshki, drank beer. My poems were filled with personal pain. I tried to make them beautiful and interesting. That is, I tried to be artful about my limited but particular experience with pain. Eventually I would modify my goals. Instead of aiming to give beautiful expression to pain, I discharged my wrath, less the beauty. Then humor against the wrath. Finally form began to matter, and so to materialize. Not to a terminal pitch, but as a conveyance, an ambulance, to carry the wounded toward where we might hope to recover from whatever afflicted us, or at least toward where we might rest from the forces. So you see, for me it is not a blasphemy, at least no blasphemy intended, when I say, I look to poetry for supernatural help.

Whether I can get away with what I write and withstand the vicissitudes and contradictions of my own character, I can't forecast. If I don't, better writers than I definitely will.

The division between urban and rural is the only serious border left to us. One serves to undermine the other. One could just as easily serve to mine the other. I am a serious border-crosser. I like the sticks; I am, if you will, of the sticks. I like the wreckage of New York City second only to the sticks of Arkansas. I am mostly a spectator at the Friday-night fights of poetics. I return to the preserve of the white page hungover. I wake up slowly. I wake up almost ready. I make myself ready.

I seek to be pulled up by my hair roots. Isn't it so with all who work with this dug-in art?

I poetry. I write it, study it, read it, edit it, publish it, teach it... Sometimes I weary of it. I could not live without it. Not in this world. Not in my lifetime. I also arkansas. Sometimes these verbs coalesce. Sometimes they trot off in opposite directions.

Concerning Complexity

I submit: the more our lives are governed by the great mix-master of egotistic, material, and technostructural forces, the more distorted the whole business of living and creating becomes;

to be undone by a work of art nowadays I seek a transient clearing in which I am compelled to rely on next to no references; I have to find it on my own and I may or may not choose to share it, so fearful I am of someone trying to stuff my wee opening with pre-frozen servings of praise and censure;

I am still wanting to get my eyes peeled by what they alone are seeing and my hair pulled by what its individual roots are feeling and my mind bent by the weirdness of its wiring,

and I am at the exact same location with regard to making anything resembling art, subordinating itself to the nomenclature of poetry, anyone calling oneself called to write poems amid all the earth noise we're putting out there;

my relationship to art changes, and I would not have it fixed;

for example I recall I didn't like Mr. Donald Judd's work until about ten years ago; then I started finding when I was in a big name-brand museum my entire anticipation was built around getting to those boxes; they just seemed to be enough;

I saw them as whole, selfless, and quite useless except to
behold; that is all and that equals an eyeful,

and I could name a few living poets who currently strike that
tone with me, but I won't not right now as I am feeling protec-
tive of and protected in their spaciousness,

and that is a space I aspire to occupy, that whatever space
I might come to take up in my own book of books should have
a singing inside;

it is not that complexity is overrated, but it is overcomplicated;
it is not that obscurity is too obscure, it's that the underside
grows grungy if it isn't exposed to a change of air;

it is not that the language is exhausted, it is that we run down;
it's not that the edge won't cut anymore, it is that the cuts are
getting thinner;

it's not that art is artificial, it is that the artists get outright
seditty; it's not that literary reputations are not inevitable,
it's that they are invented;

not that theories are not beautiful, but that they are feeble;

although we have opposable heads the legions of poets com-
posing our blue sheets will have to orchestrate the lucid inter-
vals and be prepared to fill them with eye-peeling, hairpulling,
mind-bending language,

and don't even get me started on form,

but if I were an engineer I am sure I would want to have built
the Brooklyn Bridge even if it half-paralyzed me as it did the
builder;

the mere mention of which sends me to Rockbridge County
where there's a photographer who sees the cleavage in the
ground; she sees the writing in the trees; she sees the light in
the blackwater, the trunk leaking, the columns disappearing;

down the road in Monroe there is another who can throw her
blackdrop up over the door to the death chamber and render
the map in the back roads of a face nailbright;

there's a poet in the desert who tweezes the glittering particu-
lars of the species from mounds of dead cells and arranges
them along the hairline fractures of our souls

(if there are such immanences);

in Montreal there's a long tall poet who quit her job at the
trainlines "to receive the calibration of air in the immense hall
of the station";

then there are the stalwart Waldrops;

there is never time to sort it all out so some of us get laggard;

just at the rarest opportunity to shift deeper into the some-
what miraculous, we hit the wrong-answer button; we turn
our slender chances into drool;

just when we thought we were being conducted to a single
point for a specially set-aside purpose;

it is not so complicated but it is never so simple, either;

I like to come and go through different doors more than I like
to throw my weight against the same one every time only to
discover it was hollow as Hollywood or never even locked,

and I like to change the locks once in a while, too; but it isn't
just about keeping it interesting for Author, Author or Dear
Reader;

it is about how differently things actually play out if you come
and go by different portals, long live la difference; as for tran-
scendence, well baby, that is the sun's job.

only the crossing counts.

It's not how we leave one's life. How go off
the air. You never know, do you. You think you're ready
for anything; then it happens, and you're not. You're really
not. The genesis of an ending, nothing
but a feeling, a slow movement, the dusting
of furniture with a remnant of the revenant's shirt.
Seeing the candles sink in their sockets; we turn
away, yet the music never quits. The fire kisses our face.
O phthisis, O lotharian dead eye, no longer
will you gaze on the baize of the billiard table. No more
shooting butter dishes out of the sky. Scattering light.
Between snatches of poetry and penitence you left
the brumal wood of men and women. Snow drove
the butterflies home. You must know
how it goes, known all along what to expect,
sooner or later... the faded cadence of anonymity.
Frankly my dear, frankly my dear, frankly

There is as much enmity in this starry field as in any other. Once in a great while, the susurrus of grass steers your thinking — upward.

Alliances raise important questions regardless of whether they propose palatable solutions. Enemies are energizing but that fuel is short-lasting.

I am suggesting that the radical of poetry lies not in the resolution of doubts but in their proliferation, in an ongoing interrogation with what Roberto Juarroz called the poet's one untranslatable song.

I do not know if I am trying to do something new, but I know that I am trying to learn something new. The doors fling themselves open.

Follow the lights in your own skull.

If you are so afraid of ending up with an opinion, afraid it will color your work, you might ask yourself how transparent is your refusal to make choices, how disinterested can any work be and still stand. How obvious is your withdrawal. What is the artistic advantage of neutrality, allowing such a condition even existed. How would it be distinguished from indifference or mere self-interest.

I am subject to many winds.

I am fortunate to be from the Ozarks. My family is there. My original family. I am glad for that. The trees are there. The trees true me. I hear from journalists in the state of Arkansas that the present policy of the national forestry service is to chainsaw the redbuds and dogwoods in the forest, then to poison the open stumps to create a more uniform woodland. The poison then runs off. Uniformity, in its motives, its goals, its far-ranging consequences, is the natural enemy of poetry, not to mention the enemy of trees, the soil, the exemplary life therein.

By Jude Jean McCramack
Goddamnit to Hell Dog's Foot,

The Unappeasable Mrs. Vittitow: I was seventeen when I met her. She is the one who made me want to be a writer more than any other living one. There were of course The Great Dead. They made me want to write, but failed to persuade that I could be one among writers. And the Judge, himself a great reader and wordwright. But a lawyer, a judge, and at bottom, negative to the imagination. And school, which neither aided nor abetted, nor did it crib, crab, or contain. If I were among writers customarily asked, if anyone were interested in what kind of mud I was made or whose thunder I stole, I would point to her.

That's her. Solid silver straight hair, in a thick-banged Dutch cut. Probably a towhead to start with, all her offspring were towheads. Bad posture. Double-jointed. Eyes set a little too close. Like a Siamese cat's. The very same blue as a Siamese cat. Nothing in her icebox but Hershey's Kisses, and that is no exaggeration. After work she picks up a White Castle burger. Eats something green once in a blue moon. She would much rather smoke than eat. Always in loose-fitted cotton chemise and pants. Black or bone to be the more invisible. Also because she is classical as well as poor. Mrs. Vittitow—I would not say of her—there is anything she would die for now, but I can say there is something she risked her life for once, and some would conclude that she lost.

Her first memory is of a racial incident: "I am sitting in a tub in an old kitchen. It's the farm. Wordan is washing my back. 'Nigger you got soap in my eye,' I must have said. 'Miss Hannah, Miss Margaret done called me a nigger,' Wordan must have said. I hear a German voice, my grandmother's,

'Wash her mouth out with soap.' And he did, and to this day I hate Ivory soap. It enrages me.' She was close to four, dating by the new 1936 Chrysler her father brought home moments after her mouth was soaped. She does not know where she learned the slur but it would not issue from her again.

Exactly thirty years later, a housebound mother of seven, Mrs. Vittitow experienced the freedom afforded by a car of one's own, and literally drove it to the end of the line in a campaign against white oppression in Forrest City, Arkansas. Though the town was named for the man responsible for the railroad contract that spawned its development, there is no irony in the fact that General Nathan Bedford Forrest was the first grand wizard of the Ku Klux Klan. The events of Vittitow's drive, which include a bitter boycott of white businesses; her husband's radio-broadcast repudiation of her activities; a poor people's march to Little Rock, white riots, the torching of her car in the local police station parking lot; a deputized escort out of state — strike the keynotes of a life in which my hero has always been an embroiled participant, refusing again and again the role of tragic player that the consequences of her involvement might suggest. An image of her walking the rest of the distance — across the Mississippi River bridge (the state line halves the bridge), shorn of husband, children, house, and pocketbook, toward the Memphis skyline — peers from an old residence hotel pane in my mind.

At every juncture, her life has been riveting — not only when an *Arkansas Gazette* stringer, a band of Feds, and a heavily armed white citizenry were obsessed with her daily doings. If her grandfather had not lost their Kentucky farm gambling on dogfights, she would have been landed gentry. This she dates with characteristic irony — two months before Roosevelt declared a moratorium on farm mortgage foreclosures. The house she remembers as Hopper-like, gaunt. But it was a bona fide spread complete with outbuildings, animals, woods, tennis courts — and she has lived in bona fide poverty ever since. Of her mother there are no memories since she died of cancer when Margaret was three. She was to be raised by aged and remote adults: a severe grandmother, an errant Swiss grandfather; the servant named Wordan who was born on the farm, son of a slave; her Irish father, an all-but-silent alcoholic, and her mother's sister whom her father eventually married. She recalls giving her lunch money away in kindergarten — anything to nab the attention of other children. Her eyes would go to theirs as if a string were connecting them.

Books were her defense against a wall of adults. It is among Vittitow's odd literary claims that Oscar Wilde perverted her. She read Alcott and *A Girl of the Limberlost. The Golden Bough* opened doors, though she read, she claims, without understanding. Her house held the Harvard Classics; she read out of them. The set was missing the third volume of English poets but she read Swinburne in the Sacred Heart Library. Browning she reacted against because he was her father's favorite. The Brontës, Austen, Galsworthy, Cellini's *Autobiography* ("I love it when he is forgiven for all murders past and to come"). Cyril Cusack came to her school to lecture on Hopkins. *Macbeth* came one year as did an all-girl production of *Julius Caesar.* She was smitten with Marc Antony. She memorized Cardinal Wolsey's speech. And recalls being shepherded into the auditorium to watch General MacArthur on a little snowy television mounted onstage. She was raised on heavy guilt and Catholicism. Seven months pregnant in her freshman year at Nazareth College, she could no longer conceal her condition and dropped out. Sex education was taught her by a botany teacher who pulled the shades down to tell them about chromosomes. "Christ," the botanist insisted, "had only twenty-three and he was the spit and image of his mother." Thus parthenogenesis had its exponent in Kentucky. It is a truism to say Mrs. Vittitow is a radical, an upstart, and an autodidact, but it is more honest to say she was educated to an important degree by the Ursuline nuns who pressed a sense of justice on her through the law of antithesis, and a love of literature through the parochial canon. It should also be manifest, hers is an insatiable mind.

I was seventeen when I met her. A friend in my dormitory, Cecelia Grubmeyer, had grown up next door to Mrs. Vittitow and was fully aware of her genius. V was playing poker and drinking bourbon. It was midday. Her kids were swarming. Sam, one of the twins, was rocking wildly a few inches from the blasting television. Vittitow was chasing broadsides against the Church and all instances of pretense, hypocrisy, and bigotry that had recently fallen on her ears (helped along by Jack Daniels and a losing hand). The slow burn. She monitored her children with the eyes in the back of her head. There were uncanny, utterly contextualized references to Joyce, Hopkins, Waugh, Greene, Merton, O'Connor — she knew all of the Catholic writers. That was for openers. She could quote anything — from the lyrics of "Abdul Abulbul Amir" to lengthy passages of *Ulysses;* from "The Prisoner's Letter to the Governor" to the last words of a sentry at Pompeii. Again, there was always a context, she never simply held forth. She situated.

When I was a college senior, Mrs. Vittitow lived for a time with a pot-den of us in Memphis (after we lured her away from a run-down residence hotel). We were reading Camus and Nietzsche and Dostoyevsky. Vittitow was devouring John Barth, Thomas Pynchon, and Hunter S. Thompson. It was when she was reading Pynchon that we began to call her V. Fifteen years her junior, we were reluctant to drop the courtesy title even though Mr. Vittitow had divorced her by then, and he had taken custody of the children on slippery, even insidious grounds. I made my first pale effort to write about her in a poem about a person of every possibility who lacked every opportunity and so "moved into a box with a man who fixed clocks, fixed clocks, fixed clocks."

Joe Vittitow was a television repairman. In his prime he held one fortunate job as a technical rep with Philco. They sent him to Fort Churchill on the Hudson Bay during the International Geophysical Year. They were shooting rockets into the aurora borealis. He loved it, but the work lasted only six months. Throughout their ill-matched married years he passed his evenings building model airplanes in the shed behind their house. He and Mrs. Vittitow had seven offspring, but not the thinnest string connecting their vision.

V is now ensconced in a cooperative building in Hell's Kitchen. She is among the people responsible for the community garden across the street from that building, now a city park. Finally she lives in the one place in America where a brilliant, provocative, passionate woman is not apt to be ostracized for those rare qualities — New York City. In fact a walk down Forty-eighth Street and through the garden with V is like being on Cleopatra's barge. I mean, recognition.

When I met Mrs. Vittitow in 1967 I was convinced that Arkansas was the center of the universe, that the house V occupied was the center of Arkansas, that the poker table was the center of the house, and that V was the Buddha. Omphalos. I have since seen her lose control over everything from her children to her bladder. I have never had a second's doubt but what my original revelation was genuine. When I talked to her on the phone, telling her I wanted to write a personal history of her and was thinking of using her grandfather's curse as a working title, she said she had a better one, better curse, that is, Irish: "May she marry a ghost and bear him a kitten and may the High King of Glory promise her to get the mange."

She seemed amenable to recounting the siege of Forrest City, and has saved the documentation for that eventuality.

For her, her whole history has significance only in terms of that moment, when her life was at risk. I am reminded of Yeats — a poet she knows thoroughly — on the advent of the real muse who comes with "The Circus Animals' Desertion":

> Character isolated by a deed
> To engross the present and dominate memory.

Almost none of the poetries I admire stick to their labels, native or adopted ones. Rather, they are vagrant in their identifications. *Tramp poets*, there you go, a new label for those with unstable allegiances.

Narrative *is.* You have to know when to enter in, when to egress, when to provoke, when to let be, be. However, narrative is overly identified with Southern poetry, whereas it is a life-long, global condition not a literary convention. Poets should be willing to exploit the rind of narrativity, and be more than willing to be lost at the heart. Exceptional intellection is being exercised to decry narrative. I am not learning much from that line of refutation.

Never deprive the reader of opportunities for multiple exegeses.

If there is any particular affinity I have for poetry associated with the South, it is with idiom. I credit hill people and African Americans for keeping the language distinct. Poetry should repulse assimilation. Each poet's task is to fight their own language's assimilation. Miles Davis said, "The symphony, man, they got seventy guys all playing one note." He also said, "Those dark Arkansas roads, that is the sound I am after." He had his own sound. He recommended we get ours.

Nor is the behavior of one's expression desirably static.

I am not convinced poetic camps serve the purpose of nonassimilation as well as they purport. I think they just put more heavy-handed poetry cops on the beat. They jump down your throat for commingling and they jump down your throat for having a good time and learning a new step and they jump down your throat for moving a few rocks out of your way. I have always acceded to poetry as a free space. "I'll let you be in my dream if I can be in yours." Bob Dylan said that.

The urge toward monumentation in poetry has always been funereal at best — how the maker is to be remembered, not how the making is to be achieved, not how the poem is to be discerned, not who will sense its percussion. A participatory corps is required.

For limited periods I like being lost. Perdition per se is not an obstacle to achieving something beneficial I cannot quite name.

Regarding omission: As Céline nailed the weightiest narrative under his ellipses, as Greek tragedians wrote the critical scenes to be performed offstage, as the farmer who kept his diary for fourteen years might enter a rare *Nothing happened today,* one must maintain a vigilant sense of when to leave off. When to skip. When to depart. Abjure. Leap. When to let the inferences fly. Rarely should a writer stop at a pre-destination. It is the quality of omission or suppression I believe which determines the quality and degree of a reader's participating in the telling — what inheres that the reader alone can render active and integral to it. A longtime favorite of mine is but a fragment from Sappho, adapted by Pound under the title "Papyrus":

> Spring.......
> Too long......
> Gongula......

If you know Gongula is a woman's name, you know enough.

What landscape is: not a closed space, not in fact capable of closure. With each survey the corners shift. Distance is the goal; groping, the means.

Imagine flying in concrete.

What elegy is, not loss but opposition.

By any means necessary being the only directive I can adhere to with any consistency. Some hillbilly crank or sex pistol must have already said as much.

The artistic reward for refuting the received national tradition is liberation. The price is homelessness. Interior exile.

Poetry and advertising (the basest mode of which is propaganda) are in direct and total opposition. If you do not use language you are used by it. If you do not recognize the terms *peacekeeper missile* and *preemptive strike* as oxymorons, your hole has already been dug.

Regardless of specific subject poem by poem, human experience is partly, not wholly, political. How can language, unless it avoids experience, avoid the political weather wherein it launches? Politics in an ongoing state is not a subject but an aspect.

Like serious poetry, serious political discourse is carried on in a contained, nearly entropic, environment. Being an American poet I resent that the only exhortations allowed to air nationwide are those uttered by greedheads, warheads, and other vicious throwbacks that assault the language in order to assail the earth.

I know who poetry can't accommodate: the tourist. I don't mean it is necessarily more highborn than shell art, though the effort, the ardor of it goes toward being borne up. But I believe it can't be identified with the compulsion to shop instead of the desire to touch, be touched. *Emblems of a Season of Fury:* "How should he [the tourist] realize that the Indian who walks down the street with half a house on his head and a hole in his pants, is Christ? All the tourist thinks is that it is odd for so many Indians to be called Jesus." Thomas Merton.

Just Looking:

The scene is generally uninhabited, but someone has been here—here a shed the wind left standing; here the earth scored by water, drought, or vehicle. A ladder disappears over a gargantuan hedge. Surely the hedge has been manicured since the beginning of time. Stones have composed themselves for a nonexistent ritual, and behind them the sky is moving every which way. Or: a face floats toward us in a fresco; hands appear and are intercepted by a serrated whiteness, and a figure of salt pushes his burden underground—evermore. Of course the mark of an earthling is disturbing. But the feelings provoked by human intervention are countered by the unstinting splendor of the visible.

The photographer plans ahead—not in the sense of a scheduled shoot at a designated site. He loads his car with equipment and maps, camping gear, audio tapes, trail mix, and makes an expedition of his art. He can get what he sees without getting out of the car if he chooses. If he steps inside a building, every feature bares its essential anatomy. Still, he says, the photographing is the hardest part. Craft is second skin. He took his first pictures, of a broom, when he was twelve, and was printing for Aaron Siskind a decade later.

Between the developing and the fixing of the print, beautiful but unearthly shapes arise; earthen colors are coaxed out of chemicals—red-brown from selenium, deep brown from sulfide, blue-grey and pale red from gold chloride. Painting with fixer and the tonalities latent in sensitized paper. Denny Moers is not secretive about his methods, but no one else seems to be engaging them. In fact, he cannot duplicate an image himself. The process neither static nor even stable. Every development and stage thereof is rich with the anticipation of what he will see next. And what he will do to the image once in view. Thus: a cataclysmic tree fills an eerie space; an alien form crashes the horizon.

The eye of the line (the line of the eye): Every eye sees otherwise. The shape of the object is the result—what impinges upon the sighted field; what penetrates the site itself.

Mei-mei Berssenbrugge's line lets out a translucent strand to the horizon, sometimes stretched taut and sometimes meandering as one of the hundreds of nameless arroyos. The long line sustains the visual tone—disinterested, capacious, extending. Her mind's seeming certainty in the face of the inscrutable. But this takes some working out, some elaboration, and qualifying—the shortest distance between *a* and *b* won't satisfy this line of abstraction, the seen modified by the unseen; the known by the unknowable. The language of the eye intercepting the sadness of beauty, the loneliness of space, the toll of time. The longer her sentence the more variants in its turns/breaks—prepositional phrases, compounds, subordinate clauses—creating enjambments, reversals, pauses essential to the accumulation of thought. The land mass builds up, is worn, and flattened to create a hard plane of surface that features the sky. Sky refracted against mesa, and between these two mediums, the language by which she knows them. This doesn't begin to contend with the oracular quality of her sentencing, which is ahistorical, unaccentuated, suspended as if by light alone.

When it is progressing at its best, one labors absorbed. This is the way it is, regardless of whether the work itself is going visibly well, regardless of how monotonous it obviously is to drill the same hole 120 times; cut 120 flawless hardwood strips, neatly numbering the pieces with a solder, so the cat can't disassemble them beyond restorability. Absorbed: the light leaves, temperature falls. Suddenly she is hungry, her back aches or her head hurts. At its best, the work is not in time, certainly not in the sense that most of us experience repetitive activity for little pay and less recognition. It is deep inside the lost forest of its making.

Some have said it was the sound that they liked best about *The Passenger*, the rub of a fan, a television airing through a door. Or the disjunction of sound — something is heard, e.g., a scrap of dialogue; then, what was heard is shown. Also the absence of so much talk coupled with the absence of a score. Others admire its sandy beauty, the constant sun. The mystery and suspense of it. Antonioni's characteristic psychological intensity. At least one critic dubbed it pretentious and tedious. Another jabbed at the director's thirst for purposefulness. In fact it is a very balanced film: the right measure of erotica and cerebration, suspicion and conviction, coincidence and missed connections, principle and pleasure; the right blend of light, heat, and noise. Encore.

Begin with nothing, remote starting point, the area of darkest color. Begin with nothing, which is yourself, Eternal Stranger, the poem that always acts alone. The poem supplies its references from its own surround. Sounds its own memory. The mind of the poem passes along interior surfaces. One does not contact the poem's ground without feeling bound to its secrecy. Its spans reach in both directions; they appear as tangible lengths across an opening. They attach to neither side. They duplicate themselves. And you, who are nothing, are duplicated on them. Moving. Dizzy with motion and altitude, but unafraid. See, it is just as you imagined it would be. And everything we have known, which is nothing, lines up, as do our friends, who are immanent in the lustrous element of the bridges themselves. And we who are nothing, along with everything we have known, which is nothing, have learned to listen so deeply, we have learned to say it with *silence our native tongue;* with a fluency that distributes both sound and light just so, until there is no horror vacui left in us. The unfathomable emptiness, negation, loss, absence have themselves become filling if not fulfilling. The poem is not given to nattering punctuation; the coextensive conjunction. W.S. Merwin's "The Bridges" never fails to remind me of Glenn Gould's pronouncement: "The purpose of art is not the release of a momentary ejection of adrenaline, but a gradual lifelong construction of a state of wonder and serenity."

Anything could happen in the unrequited cities of the mind.

W.S. Merwin's line has mutated several times from the early formal books, the open form of the second round of books, the grand caesura of the next round, and the increasingly dense yet translucent narratives of the later titles. His movement between narrative and lyric has been continuous. With *The Folding Cliffs,* the epic enters the corpus of his poetry, allowing the plenum of his narrative and lyric skills to, as it were, unfold. The opening line begins with the gerund *climbing.* The story is in motion. The line requires no punctuation other than capitalization and sometimes dashes. Alternate lines indent; they turn in and roll. They emerge from the mountain of the poem; they pour over the rocks. They irrigate the entire. And the entire is an island, a world unto itself. There are seven titled sections and six of them have forty numbered passages; one has forty-one. The sections and numbered passages are equivalent to chapters and scenes though they run very little interference — for it is the impetus of the line to continue without rest as the characters are forced to continue without resting. The line and the characters carried by it must not stop. The pacing is controlled in part by the carefully measured cadence of the sentencing, which keeps you abreast with the characters, their story, and does not cause you to stumble or fall out of the line. The pace is controlled in lesser degree by the titled sections, which provide the reader with trail markers, and the space between numbered sections, which provides opportunity to catch the breath. But the latter are external controls and they operate somewhat as a map's legend, letting you know your position according to scale. Allowing you to stop when you must, and resume when you can. Ideally it would be read without interruption as the sentence can sustain you through such a reading, and the narrative is that compelling. The line beckons you to stay with it. "The way is in the feet."

Just Looking:

Light permeating color, intensity modified by tone, and design ordered by scale. A sense of wakefulness, of being present for what you're looking at to reveal itself in more absolute terms... The total picture should cast back light.

That the optical source of the light be expressed as coming from within. Every picture with a *felt life*. And nuance. If fifteen layers of paint are applied — that the weave remain visible; if only one is allowed to graze the surface — that the paint stay wholly committed to the canvas. Texture built up where insisted upon, but never for its own sake. Neither excess nor washout.

Practically speaking every image has to be contained and the design respect the boundaries whether effortlessly or reluctantly. And while the images be thoroughly executed in the given spaces — that they should continue to burn not so much beyond as through the borders.

until words turn to moss.

This was all roses, here, where an overblown house crowns
the hill, the whole field, roses, all the way to the end;
when the rosarian died, the partition of roses
began. We've come out of nowhere, literally,
nowhere, autumnal towns marked for destruction
by a phantom hand; houses held underwater, every bed
a sunken tub, tools drowned between rows, every keyhole
caulked; clouds hallucinating girls asleep on a wedge
of wedding cake; the white rose, among the greatest of liars,
beginning to show the debilitating effects of fame;
the ever-popular blaze placates a vase; the bad sons
of thunder beating back a strand of light; someone
who knows nothing apart from the rain
standing on a chair in muddy legs; the roses
blown into their cumulonimbi,
and someone whose glove is recovered, a face
that doesn't come clear, a face drawn under an umbrella,
beautiful, charcoal, beautiful, like words
that never get old, the sons of thunder beating

Collaborating

with Deborah Luster: we fall in and out of step with each
other's projects without much inducement. We spring from
the same hills and hardwoods, the same thicket of teeth and
tongues. We took classical dance and mime and poetry to-
gether. We waitressed at the D-Luxe. We spelled each other
floundering and outgrowing some of our worst inclinations on
the side of hope, kinship, and expression that would suppose a
shape to otherwise unsustainable futures of anger, isolation,
and aimlessness. We think the same things are funny, the
same things wrong, and the exact same stuff un-for-get-table.

Part of my interest runs to the surface, and the framing of
that surface. On the other hand I work toward an interiority
that speaks to my own hunger. Every medium has its own lines
of influence, just as they all have common underpinnings.
Working with a filmmaker would be very different from
working with someone who makes still images. This way I
make the movable parts.

Some say form is the primary poetic value; some say, the creation of new forms is the sole business of the art. "Indeed, can there be a new thought in an old form," Fanny Howe doubted. I think the potentiality of the art resides in form.

Almost anything can, will, and does happen in an Erin Mouré line. Punctuating to the max: she ironizes words and phrases with quotation marks, quotes directly; changes point sizes and font styles, shifts back and forth between French and English. Jarringly she capitalizes and de-caps, deploys ampersands, asterisks, footnotes; also numbers and fractions. Then distributes parenthetical remarks throughout as well as actual commentary on the text she is authoring. She anticipates a critique and responds to it in advance. The line is so contrary it can manage the asides and any variety of marginalia. The marginalia insist on being key players in the action of the poem. She indicates where photos should be pasted, draws, strikes through lines. The line is searching. It is on maneuvers. It will not be still. And it keeps us alert if not agitated. Is the line going to make a sharp turn here, leave the page, or stop without warning? Will we be unceremoniously thrown off the page? Can we avert our eyes? All this pyrotechnic energy disarms us. We want to know what's next. We lean forward, into the poem. We are dealt subversion. We are also dealt into the conventions of other genres and media, including the assertions of newspapers, the iconography of popular culture, the cuts of film, the theorizing of academe, the asides of fiction and theater, and so forth. The poet's sense of inclusivity is as developed as her sense of exclusivity, and with both strategies in operation at once, there is a whole lot of shaking going on.

When I get off work, run down the unlit stairs swaddled in my twelve-foot, still-damp scarf, and swinging my helmet by the strap, my moped is gone. I bought it secondhand from a man who bought it for his wife. When she became pregnant he sold it out from under her. Now stolen from under my window at The Poetry Center. The twenty minutes it took to get back to Potrero Hill turns into an hour and twenty. It is the end of the streetcar line. But I can still meet Forrest for stir-fried, who is already home, working on his breathless poem "Rush to the Lake." But no, that poem comes later, after we watch the tail end of a silent movie in the lobby of an out-of-the-way hotel in Mexico City. "The Last Castrato" would be written there too, the first poem he wrote that I love. Breathless poems. Written in Mexico. Maybe we can take in a ten o'clock movie at the Roxie. I can undo my pack on the ride to my dingy apartment on Potrero Hill, take out a notebook and make an entry.

For decades the critical question has been, Can poetry survive? Is it mutable, profound, sentient, resplendent, intense, stalwart, brave, alluring, exploratory, piercing, skillful, percipient, risky, exacting, purposeful, nubile, mirth-provoking, affective, restive, trenchant, sybaritic, nuts enough? Can it still enkindle, prod, or enlarge us? And even if yes, yes to all of the above, is it enough? Among poets this inquiry is persistent. And if the answer is nay, all this and more is not enough, the question becomes, With what then will we hail the next ones, the ones who have to pick up around here long after we've been chewing the roots of dandelions?

I do not know how a southerly lyric might express itself, at least in terms of definition, but I am attempting to initiate my own practice of the same. "One does what one knows before one knows what one is doing." I think Charles Olson said that.

I was born in a warren of no great distinction in the vicinity of the middle hillbilly class. There, with progressive effort (gravity never sleeps), I will possibly grow quite old (the women do in my family), and indisputably shall I die. I am the daughter of an annually retired judge who has lived and worked inside the tawny leather bindings of jurisprudence for well over half a century. For this man words themselves have become palpable, material, and even law. And I am the daughter of a woman whose manipulations of the stenotype machine, crossword puzzle, and telephone have likewise been exhaustively verbal. Both of them are autochthons of the rural Arkansas Ozarks. The paternal side issues from a farming community named Cisco that no longer salaries a postal clerk to raise our country's flag (nor has it since the flag wore forty-nine stars). The distaff side hails from the bluffs of a beautiful swift river in a moribund railroad town whose rock buildings have been mortared back into service by a German manufacturer of work uniforms.

It is poetry that remarks on the barely perceptible disappearances from our world such as that of the sleeping porch or the root cellar. And poetry that notes the barely perceptible appearances.

It falls on the sweet neck of poetry to keep the rain-pitted face of love from leaving us once and for all.

Formal options are virtually unlimited; one has to train oneself to recognize and utilize them, as well as discover and rediscover them. It is the fit lexicon for one's preoccupations that is elusive; it is the preoccupations themselves that have to be transmuted into considerations larger than the mind they occupy.

In the past two years I have published several screeds regarding the defenestration of poetry, expelling in the process much of my own frustration. Once on the outside it has not had the same gaseous effect. Inside, it burned odorlessly, colorlessly, while I worked and while I slept. Nobody reads poetry, we are told at every inopportune moment. I read poetry. I am somebody. I am the people, too. It can be allowed that an industrious quantity of contemporary American poetry is consciously written for a hermetic constituency; the bulk is written for the bourgeoisie, leaving a lean cut for labor. Only the hermetically aimed has a snowball's chance in hell of reaching its intended ears. One proceeds from this realization. A staggering figure of vibrant, intelligent people can and do live without poetry, especially without the poetry of their time. This figure includes the unemployed, the rank and file, the union brass, banker, scientist, lawyer, doctor, architect, pilot, and priest. It also includes most academics, most of the faculty of the humanities, most allegedly literary editors and most allegedly literary critics. They do so — go forward in their lives, toward their great reward, in an engulfing absence of poetry — without being perceived or perceiving themselves as hobbled or deficient in any significant way. It is nearly true, though I am often reminded of a Tranströmer broadside I saw in a crummy office building in San Francisco:

> We got dressed and showed the house
> You live well the visitor said
> The slum must be inside you.

If I wanted to understand a culture, my own for instance, and if I thought such an understanding were the basis for a lifelong inquiry, I would turn to poetry first. For it is my confirmed bias that the poets remain the most "stunned by existence," the most determined to redeem the world in words...

At reading I excelled from an early age, and at writing I estivated. By the time I resolved to stir and apply myself to the page, I was afraid it was too late. Not that I was a sloth, but I was an ignoramus. I am uncertain about the former but there is remedy for the latter. According to Simone Weil, "One is never got out of the cave, one comes out of it." Like my father and my mother before me, I put every cent of my stock in the word. A few carelessly set mental fires: a house strewn with books, a Mississippi history teacher's recitation of "Buffalo Bill's defunct"; a self-taught friend's addiction to Irish, English, and American poetry, and a fateful encounter with a poet my age who wrote in a lexicon known to the marrow of my bones, lit for me, poetry.

I admire poetry that confutes its own formal conditions — poetry that due to the exigence of its own matter exceeds its own limits. Some of us do not read or write particularly for pleasure or instruction, but to be changed, healed, charged. Therefore, the poet's amplitude may take precedence over her strategies. When aiming for a language nearer one's own ideals and principles, a tongue wherein everything is at risk — there are no certainties. This has been dubbed *unimproved* poetry. *Untrammeled* is Merwin's stately word for the poem's inalienable right to freedom. The French formalists, known as Oulipo (*L'Ouvroir de Littérature Potentielle*), name it pejoratively *shriek* poetry or *eructative* poetry. *Unfettered* was Kurt Schwitter's turn-of-the-twentieth-century word. The punks could have called it *thrash* poetry. Oh yeah.

Regarding the territorial conflicts of urban intellectuals, I admit a gauge of relief going back to the hills where writers and nonwriters alike are more practically delineated. Flannery O'Connor divided people into only two classes: the irksome and the non-irksome, without regard to sex. Her refinement included the medium-irksome and the rare-irksome.

I would like to insert here that just as I reject the notion of a politically neutral poetry, I reject the notion that certain concerns evidently appropriate to one genre are therefore inappropriate to another — a chair is not a lamp is not a toaster... This is another unnecessary limitation. The foil of expertism.

At the formal fringe of free verse, the design is there, the analysis has been wanting.

In the first sentence of "The American Rhythm," Mary Hunter Austin's early 1900s essay, rhythm is equated with experience. Physiologically she locates rhythm "in the dimension of appreciable stress," and according to Austin, "the only indispensable condition for the acquirement of new rhythms and their use, is that the points of stress recurrence should lie within the normal stress capacity of the organism"; that is, "within the limits of pleasurable exercise." On the first level of experience, she identifies the major rhythms as those dictated "by the blood and the breath." Then those that satisfy the organism's social, ego, and mating urges. Such rhythms she describes as instinctive, and thus habitual responses or those of which the initiative is lost. "Being lost," Austin asserts, "is one of the conditions of our making poetry of it." After which, "new rhythms are born of new motor impulses"; "true evocation is from the autonomic centers of *experience.*" In Austin's view nothing was more inevitable than that American poets would "overwhelm" the European verse models, "given a new earth to live on, new attacks on the mastery of time and space, a whole new scale of motor impulses is built into the subconscious structure... Whatever Russ and Pole and Serb had come to America for," she writes, "it wasn't at least that they might learn to express themselves in pentamic hexameter." She continues to elaborate not only the grand examples of Whitman and Lowell, but to advance an ardent ethnographic assay of expressive Native American rhythms:

> One winter at Tesuque I saw the Eagle dancers on a windy day catch up the rhythm of the wind through the tips of their wind-spread plumes and weave it into the pattern of their ancient dance, to the great appreciation of the native audience. After twenty years' observation, it remained for Ovington Colbert, a Chickasaw, to point out to me that the subtle wavering of the movement of

the Squaw Dance, which I had supposed to be due to the alternate relaxation and tension of interest, was really responsibly attuned to the wind along the sagebrush.

With the same inspired accuracy, Mary Austin describes other subordinate rhythms such as those set by "a bandeau of whispering cocoons wrapped round the torso." To the underpinning line Austin discerns in Native American poetry, she assigns the term *landscape line*, which she sees as most compatible with Amy Lowell's coinage *cadenced verse*. Austin's landscape line, like Native American poetry, is shaped "by its own inner necessities" — without disposition, according to her, to force the word into a predetermined mold. Nor does accent have a predetermined status, "apart from the natural movements of thought." Austin claims that all verse forms "found worthy [for] the use of great poets are aboriginal, in the sense that they are developed from the soil native to the culture that perfected them."

What most impressed me about Mary Austin's argument is her ability, in spite of her own background and education, to spurn the absolute authority of English fixed forms along with her skillful subjection of Native American poetry to a detailed historical and structural analysis.

It had been my own aspiration, when I first undertook to write poetry, to read and make poetry, that it would bring people together. My aspirations are still pitched high, though my expectations of it being either a source or beneficiary of this virtuous by-product have subsided. At times I am half persuaded the reasons for exhaustively articulated divisions among contemporary American poetics are real. At other times, I think they are fundamentally French. For the most part I suspect the skirmishes are pertinent to clarification, and yet more relational to our removal from the public sphere, the near total disenfranchisement of the American intellectual, eventually leading to the proverbial infighting that throttles any worthwhile effort.

Pure poetry, nonstop, it is wearing. I get so tired of the sect of poetry. I want my writing to be exploratory and animate and profound. I want to touch my blameless dreams, even if to date it is all paper and mistakes. Can anyone get there writing unadulterated poetry?

Now that I am beyond the initial paralysis of calling one's first teachings into question, I am left with: be critical and sing.

The great barrier of objectivity, it is the banal standard of professionalism.

Poetry is the language of intensity. Because we are going to die, an expression of intensity is justified.

Extended awareness, is that not central to the art?

Asked informally, "What is a young poet to do," Robert Creeley proposed, "form a company." He meant, start an e-zine or a press, publish yourselves. One press flies by the Ethernet; start another by prosaic day. Form a company in the repertory theater's sense of the word *ensemble* — let each do their part. "Each has his or her place in the procession," just as Walt said.

Zaum.

Another strategy is to create new structures that further the art (for its own sake). Create a language the unborn might be unashamed to speak.

While some writers are choosing sides, others are building intricate arches over the gorge. Laying track. Crossing the borders by dark to take what they need from the novel here, history or astronomy there, and no more. Such authors have designed new orders that allow the most aleatoric admissions to stand solidly or sleep soundly in the context of their individual works. The spirit, be it lost, if it comes to nothing and verges on perishing, thrives here, beating and constellated, among the country's clashing poets.

Poets should exceed themselves — when demands on us are slack, we should be anything but. Pressing the demands of the word forward is not only relevant but urgent. If our country does not vigorously cultivate poetry, it is either poetry's ineluctable time to wither or time to make a promise on its own behalf to put out new shoots and insist on a much bigger pot.

Give physical, material life to the words. Record what you see. Rise, walk, and make a day. Grandmother Wright oft bade the latter.

Make an entry.

Enthroned in the ergonomic chair, aligned for enhanced efficiency and productivity, one is advised to resist the amorous movement of the stippo grass; to summon what Barbara Guest dubs *orchid attention* before running to seed.

What It Is:

According to the late Frank Stanford, his introduction to the
venerable Malcolm Cowley, whom he had come to help inter-
view on film, was met with surprise bordering on suspicion.
Seeing in him an uncanny resemblance to young Hart Crane,
a photo album was produced by Mrs. Cowley that Mr. Cowley
might make the point. Also according to Frank — when the
novice poet pressed his first collection, *The Singing Knives,*
upon the famed editor, Cowley barked, "My boy, you know
what art is?" Young Stanford was quick to admit, "No sir, not
I sir." And Cowley quick to bark, "It is an ostrich, sticking its
head in the sand, shitting bricks." Followed a lengthy pause.
"Thus the pyramids."

To eliminate, from the category Art, homo-erotica is to suppress art on its primary grounds, the critical and liberating.

Back during Gulf War 1, Madonna, clothed in $20,000,000 in jewels and little else, mouthed come-ons to General Norman Schwarzkopf at the Academy Awards. In doing so she satisfied the obvious terms of the American love equation. Indeed, Madonna and Norman constitute the ideal national partnership, the media-created goddess and a heroic instrument of violence; whereas sex partnered with nonviolence is unthinkable for it might be critical or worse, liberating — it might be liberating or worse, critical.

The furor over funding for the arts provided a short-term distraction from the exigent problems of the nation as well as from its preparations for that occasion for war. The war in turn served to distract us from both the arts debate and the exigent problems of the nation. Otherwise, the arts would have received their usual pittance — overriding the customary redneck objections, but without benefit of the press. Arts funding in our country is routinely a pittance, unmatched for its meagerness among developed countries except by apartheid South Africa, another power incapable of countenancing any form of expression that did not advance institutionalized violence against its own body politic.

What had to be called into front-page question was an eidolon of a bare black body cupped against a bare white body (of the same sex). What had to be suppressed was the imminent charring of tens of thousands of bodies — kids on up — so like our own.

Fighter pilots aboard the USS *JFK* watched porno movies before their bombing missions, according to a January 1991 article in the *Washington Post*. The paper said the first report of this story by the AP was censored by the military.

As an admittedly defensive measure I have taken to my stony, garreted art for partisan relief—for some insistence upon a full life. And I have gone looking into the dungeon whence the radon seeps, where no records are kept, and lo, even under the nap of the grass, where mutations teem.

In the feverish atmosphere of post–World War II, Georgia O'Keeffe undertook to compel us to really see a calla lily. With *Odas Elementales* (1954), Pablo Neruda advised us to "look closely at the world of objects at rest. Wheels that have crossed long, dusty distances with their mineral and vegetable burdens... barrels, and baskets, handles and hafts for the carpenter's tool chest." "From them," he writes, "flow the contacts of man with the earth, like a text for all harassed lyricists." So, in Neruda's elemental odes, we stare intently into the kingdom of socks, salt, lemons... In the States it has not been the so-called confessional poets—the poets more frequently associated with lyric writing—but the objectivists who have fixed our sense on the world of objects at rest. Of the objectivists none were more devoted to "the little / thin things" in a more essential language than Lorine Niedecker:

> Asa Gray wrote Increase Lapham:
> pay particular attention
> to my pets, the grasses.

What I believe poets John Wieners and Frank O'Hara offered us toward a new ode is in part the peculiar American talent for dirtying the waters. The poem of The Court becomes the poem of The Rabble, in their splendor. The panegyrist returns to the page as author and civilian. Personhood is restored to the old authority of Poet. One's friends are welcome whether they are famous painters or merely passengers in frumpy coats. The trademark of the work is openness. And a new ode did briefly flow from this tradition.

The links between poetic strategies, tactical maneuvers including gamesmanship, and social stratification clank through time, across channels and oceans to be sure. The poetry of the white shirt does not gladly speak to the poetry of the blue. The audience, the constituency, or if you will, the *allegiance* of the cultural elite belongs to the cultural elite. One would show little thought to expect otherwise.

Nevertheless poets have periodically formed belligerent subclasses, and entered into the ranks of honorees in extremely limited numbers, usually as sole, acceptable representatives for the entire subclass. Even these ruptures cast the phantasmata of quality and value into temporary disarray. If the numbers continue to push at the limits of the established order, further subdivisions might arise at a near invisible remove from the original hierarchy. Only those whose mimicry of the elite is outstanding — though ostensibly oppositional — succeed in gaining a competing footing.

Allowing for collective effort and reliable human error, one can depend upon brief and abrupt breaks in any high-security environment. The struggle for legitimacy is as unrelenting as the vigilance required to contain it. But it is usually less systematic. And those who advance with a brilliant methodology do so at the risk of taking on traits of the very breed they would depose. One notices for instance that the charges against the opposition-identified "academic poets" dropped off as the self-identified opponents began to take up gainful employment therein.

Gertrude Stein died under anesthetic in 1946, seven years after the death of Yeats, almost a decade before Stevens's, nearly two before Frost's.

The signature of the work is her vigorous application of repetition. Beginning, middle, and ending are forsworn for the loop, the continuous present, a technique she considered cinematic. Certainly with respect to the printed word, time would never be the same After Stein. "There's joy in repetition," moans The Artist Formerly Known As Prince, known once again as Prince. "I'm not a fool," she insisted, "I know in daily life people don't go around saying a rose is a rose is a rose, but in that line the rose is red for the first time in English poetry in 100 years." She had a point. A noun "caressed and addressed" by Stein, stimulates the senses and rewards the wide-awake reader.

There is a boggling level of inclusivity in Stein, made more of a boggler given her method of composition, the ceaseless reiteration that, medically-speaking, might qualify as a syndrome. Out of this reiteration, an intensity. Out of this inclusivity, a leveling of word, phrase, and sentencing that combined to effect a vitalization of poetry in a late age. No one has equaled her exaggerated melodies, and not until another friend of the painters, Frank O'Hara, took to the streets of New York in the 1950s would there be another American poet offering a late age such immediacy, excitement, and an altogether rare literary streak of optimism.

She was a merrily errant writer. Her unfailing ear, her radical syntax, and, perhaps more than any other quality, her comfort with her own procedures set her texts securely in the foreground of American experimentalists. Stein's vocabulary is childishly simple; furthermore, literal. Her tone is naive, childishly so.

She verbalizes what she sees. But exposure of method is not disclosure of being, and behind the simple facade, a lion that never sleeps, that is devouring, and behind the lion, another facade.

If like Keats you find yourself longing to escape from a low-grade funk in which "men sit and hear each other groan," there may be a welcome breeze admitted in rehabilitating the ode.

Homo loquens, creature with the gift of tongues. It is, is it not, who we are.

In the book *Standing Wave* each stanza of "Star Dust" is on a separate page. In the book, "Star Dust" and "Alternate Take" are separated by forty pages. John Taggart connects, "one line to line with one line to line at a time." He pulls his end of the line that has no end — until he elects to nail a period firmly to its tail — from the source that has no beginning. A standing wave is one "characterized by a lack of vibration at certain points, between which areas of maximum vibration occur periodically. Standing waves are produced whenever a wave is confined within boundaries, as in the vibrating string of a musical instrument." In 1991 he published *Loop.* A loop, as we know, "is something which has a shape, order, or path of motion that is circular or curved over on itself." In electricity it is "a closed circuit." In computer science it is "a sequence of instructions that repeats itself either a specified number of times or until a particular condition prevails." Repetition dictates the duration of Taggart's line internally and externally, its cadence, breath, and break. By the very insistence of repetition, he fields the depth of sound and then its spread. He creates both circuitry and new links. One could say the poem waylays completion for the sake of extension, and that the waylay is in itself pleasing. The relation to praying, chanting, lauding, and perhaps even exorcising (as evil so often lurks) is apparent. The line in the mind is sung. The line is itself pure song. And actual songs (e.g., "Star Dust") are often invoked by title, phrasing, pitch, and spirit from the classic American bins of rhythm and blues, blues, jazz, and sorrow songs. The words, in keeping with the music of this line, hold their shape; stay simple — ear, space, room, floor, garden, boy, father, field, road, cloud cover... The song does not get stuck on specifics. The emotions won't tolerate the clutter, and the line clears the way for the emotions. The line moves, a shining ring, circulating for the forsaken, the unconsoled. "The reason was to light the light that was radiantia radiantia that was a singing light in darkness."

My story is not important, but odd like horses lying down. I am of the opinion your story is no more or less important. Just last week I took the bus to work because my car was in the shop. I transferred downtown. And not being too familiar with the lines, I prepared to get on any bus that stopped. Close to where I stood, an older woman pulled me back to the shelter of the department store overhang. "That's not your bus," she said, "I can usually tell." And this being Providence, she was right. There are those who stay below, and those who mount the hill. I was dressed to take the hill. Another sentence or two was exchanged, somehow making it possible for her to tell me: She lost her brother in the Coconut Grove fire of 1942, four hundred and ninety-two dead. Also that the rest of her family went quickly after the first death, her father within a few months. She had bought him Lucky Strikes on the evening of his death; they were fifteen cents a pack then. And he died on the couch, before pulling the red string from the cellophane. She lived, she said, in the Four Seasons. I knew she was telling

me the name of her apartment building. That she was imply-
ing that I, a stranger, might visit her there. I was as struck by
the phrase "I live in the four seasons" as I was touched by the
proposition. There are how many — two hundred and thirty
million — stories in the naked land. All unimportant, all our own.

I would be solidary with poets, but that does not mean vertical
relationships do not abound in this and every other human
enterprise, utopian, heretical, or otherwise. Realizing how
endlessly divisible one brood of poets is from another — the
ones in the white shirts from the ones in the blue from the
ones in black — I have nearly ceased thinking of poetry as a
public art, but instead as an ever-shrinking arena for cultural
conflict. Poetic theories and applications line up with pedigree
in disturbing yet ever-changing degrees. Be that as it may, poets
can still be counted on to stand nearly as one against the
abjectification of contemporary experience.

We are indispensable to one another. We keep the language
machine going — often in different directions at once. And the
behavior of language is such that parallel concerns and sym-
pathies are available to serious practitioners on many levels,
at any point in space and time — the formal, the inventive, the
revelatory, the message plane itself. I don't accept that language
transcends the material, but I do believe it is an imperfect,
maybe even rude, instrument for class transgression. The
emancipatory function of art keeps central, at least in the
mind of the practitioner.

In America money, for its own sake, is an exalted pursuit.
Money drains consciousness and courage and leaves in its
stead a virtually anal desiccation that can only be treated

homeopathically, with more upon more of the same, which is its only essential characteristic. Money holds more sway than blood in America; this is our significant departure from the European class system. The old equation that money is power is not worth disputing. Clearly, not every last member of the moneyed are consumed with power. Not every last member of the powerful are consumed with money. Some would be poets. That poetry does not overwhelm the effects of money or power is also hardly worth disputing.

Of the choices revealed to me, crime and art were the only ones with any real sex appeal. As the daughter of a judge and a court reporter, my conditioning was secular. I was protected against violence and warned against shoplifting, peeping, and cheating, but art like crime presented a charismatic, trans-gressive countenance. Out of the trash heap of language, poetry emerges rich and revolutionary, fecund and childless, genuine and artificial, deadly and peaceful. It favors the oxy-moron; that too keeps it interesting. Who would not want to be an artist once the choice took shape in the mind, and was given a minimum of encouragement to take hold.

Opportunity is so bound to choice. The opportunity to fall into the pages of a book and have one's eyes peeled by words; the opportunity to listen, learn, discern; the opportunity to move freely and deeply inside one's subject... Such options are hardly birthrights for the majority. They barely register as options for the minority of the minority. Those with no shirt — no white, no blue, no black, no uniform — have no say. And into this scene rides many a young outlaw.

My own writing careens along two vectors that do not always parallel, intersect, or coalesce. One projects itself into a provocative space. It would challenge the obnoxious privileges and prerogatives of power. It would enter that challenge as a vote against greed, apathy, chauvinism, and other virulent strains of egotism and predation. That the space is neutral is one of science's fallacies, and more than enough artists attach themselves to the claim. They should have been scientists, these neutral, disinterested ones. That artists are better examples than any other citizen, either in their work or their lives, is one of poetry's fallacies. A deplorable share of us are skillful at severing the thing-in-the-making from the made thing from the maker in much the same way that scientists have artfully severed the obvious applications of their work from its theoretical development (and from the fiscal sources of encouragement). Yet, I would submit, writing all but involuntarily pertains to consciousness. Consciousness is critical. How could it be otherwise? This is my brief.

Along the other vector, writing for me is a thing delicate as love. And one struggles (the struggle is never separate from the engagement) to be a newborn in love, to be without attributes, like snow nobody has walked on. Prelapsarian. Also to be mutable like the river that cannot be stepped in twice. Thus with one rivery exhalation of words after another, I write. To rise above one's own failures, to wrest hope from the next disappointment, to feel such clarity and happiness, to indulge in one's own fertile mind — the great rush to participate in the odyssey of language, to take up the leaky pen of a long, wended life; to lie down with "our rich friend silt." Writing: bad thoughts, bad feelings slither away one by one. This is my breviary.

Poetry for me is compatibly tendentious and personal. It is both reproachful and irresistible. It thrives on errancy (as well as an excess of pride and piety). Writing is a discretionary activity; it follows that reading is, too. Controversies between strains of poetry are useful tools of refinement, perhaps especially to those of us who see ourselves on the sidelines but affected by kindred issues. But literary hegemony, the drive to prevail, seems insupportable, and poisonously reflective of class allegiances. Both the vanguard and the rear guard simulate the dominant hierarchies. Of the vanguard I can say, I admire their procedures, but I think their attitude stinks. Of the rear guard I admit I think their procedures and their attitudes stink. When this discord erupts into an all-or-none competition, the last reader can exit in a body bag. "Writing," as Colette wrote, "leads only to writing." I do not see any end to it.

Arkansas would not prepare me for the East. In the East there are standards. Somehow it still seems to set the tone for the pedagogical wars that are going on all over the country, Manhattan excepted, which I read as a more chaotic, disinstitutionalized island of discourse. In New York City, a free-for-all of poetries stays open twenty-four hours. Some assemble by night and others by day. Recently a roving monochromatic band of nocturnals charged the offices of *The New Yorker* in the A.M. demanding to see the poetry editor, with the claim that they were just as bad as the poets she regularly published. Such a mocking confrontation is unthinkable here in New England. Here in New England it helps to come from a really good family whether headed for poetry's cutting edge or the boardroom. As with Californians, Easterners prefer to talk poetry with one another, with like-minded Californians, and with their French betters. Class, "the unmentionable five-letter word," is to an uncertain degree an inseparable dimension of aesthetic practices — exploratory, traditional, ethnic; also lyric, narrative, epic.

Electronically, geographic borders are dissolving by the nanosecond. The impact upon poetry of this universal wiring is inestimable. Interactive technology does not mean that the hierarchies of craft are becoming more permeable. It will not mediate the grounds for inclusion or exclusion. Who can walk the walk and who can talk the talk will profit in this dimension the same as in hard copy. Knowing the faultiness of my own wiring I would prefer to acquire this know-how by mouth (surely a pill is in the works), barring that, by implant.

I would see the spine of cultural power pulverize in its own bones, but not expect nor want the tensions between tendencies flattened. I would see them recast so as to be more vexing of their own composition, and more alert to relational assets.

We are the bankrupt aristocracy of letters. We wear our coat of arms with a shabby haughtiness that sometimes lands us in the company we think is our birthright, but usually leaves us to simply look down upon one another — which we manage to do with a vengeance. How dreary that it should come to this, and what fun it was to be broke in our youth. "How is it that you live, and what is it you do?" Wordsworth asked the leech gatherer, who was not the one complaining.

These then are spiritual exercises: walk don't drive, when you do drive, drive slowly, make room for the one behind you, when you drive don't read, listen; when you read, read poetry. Furthermore, if this is how you live and what you do, persevere, and gather your leeches while and where you may.

I feel complete when this trouble is shared, and when it is being made, alone, in the dark, I feel like a spider who has to get that web made because she's hungry. She is always hungry. I have a spidery hand and I try to get it to transmit to my mind, and then I try to make it attractive enough to draw others in. They say Walt Whitman's beard drew butterflies.

I like to sit around with people I like and people about whom I haven't made up my mind yet — drinking wine and eating a crazy salad with our meat, talking straight poetry. On those moonless nights it does not matter if anything is written down or not. The words burn into our brains.

There was plenty of loud talk at the table, late corn, continuous palaver in other parts of the house; a handsome brother with principles and the future on his mind, who came in good time to counsel the mentally unbalanced. None of the Wrights so far as that goes are inordinately stable. Or else, neurotically so. We are a smart bunch. Verbal down to the altogether illiterate. Nineteen forty-nine, the year stoically captioned by one poet as "a whore blowing smoke in the dark," I was born on epiphany, a podalic version. "You tore me up," my mother swore. "No more," and her womb blew back into the trees. My first words, I am told, were obscene. My high chair was handed-down and painted-over white. I remember the hard heels of my white shoes chipping at the paint of the rung. I came up in a large unaestheticized house littered with the *Congressional Record* and stenotype paper. Only girl of a Chancery Judge and the Court's hazel-eyed Reporter who took down his every word — which was law. Throughout my childhood I was knife-sharp and aquatic in sunlight. I read.

The particulars of hill society have shaped my work more than any certain somebody. Rereading the Writers' Program WPA *Guide to the State*, published first in 1941, and extrapolating from descriptions of individual hill women, I have no trouble spotting myself: bony but strong as a weed, an abiding refusal to smile or sing, relentless if not brutal honesty, streaks of the mean, the grotesque in humor. Thomas Hardy's descriptions of the peasant yeomanry of England, quoted in the same guide, are likewise faithful to my relations: "blond, grey-eyed, slim, with straight mouths, determined chins, independent and hidebound, adaptable to circumstances, free of outside influences, not complacent, and don't fight well unless cornered. Then to the death." In my family, until my parents' generation, all were dirt farmers on the father's side; railroad workers on the mother's. Both sides have taken root in the most stubborn sense of the word in similar topography for a couple hundred years: Alleghenies, Blue Ridge, Smokies, Ozarks with a scant sampling forging as far west as the Oklahoma Badlands. At the *a cappella* funeral of Great-Uncle Audie I discovered the badlands branch of the family. Audie died deliberately at the age of eighty-nine from carbon monoxide poisoning.

Five of Us Drove to Horatio:

after first picking up seven-year-old Brecht Gander from camp
on Petit Jean mountain. Once we arrived in Horatio, we phoned
the postmaster at her home (it was the weekend), and she
drove down to the gas station to meet and lead us to the
Brighams'. We brought peaches. It was hot. Their a/c didn't
work. They had cats. Around thirty of them, but one quickly
lost count. They were draped over everything. The heat and
the cat musk clobbered the senses.

In their modest living room was a modest cabinet, built for
Besmilr by Roy, to house, no, safeguard, her work. It closed
solidly. Maybe it even locked. Opened, with her standing be-
tween you and the mother lode, the shelves were jammed with
hard, black binders. Titles were printed on the spine with what
appeared to be nail polish: *To Live as a Bird, Blue Fields of the
Bell Lagoon, A Light in the Water,* etc., etc. I was beside myself.
Debbie and Mike and Forrest diplomatically coaxed her from
the house to the porch to the yard to interview and photo-
graph and film her. She accommodated us, but she didn't
indulge us. She did not like Roy to be far from her side. Nor
did she like prying eyes. In other words, she did not know who
we were, but she knew who she was.

They had owned a newspaper in a small town in Texas.
They sold it because, as she said in a 1973 interview with
Thomas Linn, "we didn't want to live that way." They never
did. They worked periodically. He set type. She taught. They
raised their daughter, Heloise. They wandered. They ensured
that Heloise attended school in Arkansas within the limits of
the law. The rest of the time, they were on their own, those
three. They were, in a bygone sense of the word, free. "We were
down in Old Mexico," she told the interviewer. "We slept where

we found a place. Where we were. We often camped and made no more than twenty-five miles a day. If we saw a beautiful tree just up the road, we would often camp again." They broke their last twenty to go to Nicaragua. When they stopped to buy a soda, a man offered to trade one hundred and eleven raincoats for their car. The man had only one hundred and nine raincoats, but he made up the difference, and the Brighams traded their car. In Nicaragua they sold the raincoats in a port town, Bluefields, that her father had once lived in for ten years working for a Boston-based mahogany company. A banana boat brought them back to the United States. "For years," Ms. Brigham told Mr. Linn, "I couldn't eat a banana." Their only child, raised thusly, came to value sitting out a storm in a café in Guanajuato talking about Victor Hugo with her parents, over being confined to a classroom in Horatio. Eventually Heloise would marry the poet Keith Wilson and they would settle in Las Cruces, New Mexico, where Keith held a professorship. They would raise five roving, hypereducated children and move Heloise's parents to Las Cruces when it became clear that the Brighams could no longer live independently.

Within the coming months, Besmilr and her husband would need to come under the full charge of their daughter and son-in-law. Soon after they moved to Las Cruces, an addition was built onto the Wilson house for them; Roy died and Besmilr had to go into a nursing home in the advancing stages of Alzheimer's. Miraculously, most of the cats were adopted. More miraculously, Roy had maintained copies as well as a detailed record of Besmilr's published and unpublished poetry and prose. So the writing is intact, a life's work.

And Besmilr wrote most of the time, most of her life. From girlhood. She recollected that if her mother told her to churn the butter, she would churn the butter then write a poem about making butter. She published a great deal during a very short period of that long writing life. In the late sixties and early seventies, there was interest in poetry by women, especially with significant claim to Native American (in her case, Choctaw) heritage. She did not really exploit either opportunity, but when work was requested, she (or more likely Roy) supplied the pages. So, one would find her represented in Mexico City–based *El Corno Emplumado,* and in *Harper's Bazaar, The Atlantic Monthly, The New York Times, New Directions* annuals, and even in Thomas Merton's short-lived *Monks Pond.* She frequently appeared in college magazines such as *Open Places* (Stephens College), *University of Tampa Poetry Review, Confrontation* (Long Island University), *North American Review* (University of Northern Iowa), and independent magazines such as *Hearse* and *The Little Review.* Canadian, Mexican, and U.S. writers often appeared together, as did city and rural poets; Southern, Midwestern, and Coastal, young and old. And though she maintained her birthdate was 1923, it was in fact 1913, and she first published in *El Corno Emplumado* in 1966. She entered print with a characteristic mixture of savvy and naïveté. Aesthetically, it was an eclectic period. The arguments were not refined. The lines were temporarily drawn, and they often intersected rather than opposed.

Brigham had a penchant for extended, serial poems, and magazine editors did not prove resistant to including them. She wrote scores of stories, and these too found their way into magazines. She graduated from the Mary Hardin-Baylor College in Texas, and attended the New School for Social Research on a scholarship. In 1970 she would be a Discovery Award winner from the National Endowment for the Arts, along with Alice Walker, Raymond Carver, Louise Glück, Lucille Clifton, Fanny Howe, Simon Ortiz, Hugh Seidman, and others. She was not ignored, but she was isolated. She corresponded with writers and editors. She knew some writers. Probably the writers closest to her personally were her son-in-law and the poet John Gould Fletcher. She was an acquaintance of Robert Duncan and of Robert Creeley. There is no question but what her literature was informed both by the European tradition and the modernists of America. Her library, stored in out-of-service appliances, was extensive. Her correspondence with writers and editors was voluminous.

Whatever literary ties are to be exposed, Besmilr Brigham was essentially on her own, with her books and her cats, with her husband and her daughter, with her own past, and with the inhuman inhabitants of the landscapes she knew best, Arkansas and Mexico. Asked by Thomas Linn why she wrote about Mexico, she replied, "There are two places I love more than any others: Mexico and Mexico." Asked why did she write poetry, she said, "I found it was a game." Then she paused. "A very serious game." She continued, "Poetry is functional with sound. We live inevitably in an abstract world. Very much we only see in the remarkable, the exaggerated. You do want it to mean something to someone else." Asked where she got her ideas, she did not hesitate: "Mexican newspapers, the library, on the radio, everywhere. It is surprising what you can find that a Spanish instructor can't tell you. We paid a boy to go to the circus if he would return and tell us what had happened. It is good to get a different viewpoint."

The writing is odd both on the surface and below, and it never quite yields its oddness however commonplace the subject. The punctuation is erratic and eccentric but deliberate. She prefers an opening parenthesis to a closing one. She is partial to the lowercase. She hyphenates nonhyphenated words to influence pronunciation and rhythm. She leaves strings of modifying words without hyphens to interject surprise and ambiguity. A backslash is often chosen internally in lieu of a line break or a caesura. The sentencing is viperine, fanged, and sometimes headless. It is unorthodox to say the least. She is not wedded to the left margin or to the stanza, but the lines usually move from the margin, and are organized in strophes.

A conclusion is rarely dramatic or conclusive. She is bent on the process, she writes *in time.*

Brigham describes what she sees, but she resolutely shortens the distance between viewer and object by a kind of poetic notation. She is a poet of the natural world not in the pastoral sense but in the habitual sense. As one reviewer put it, her poems are her five senses. Living and dying are the time-honored themes, but very much in the act of—rather, the *process* of, and always with unaverted eyes. Her identification with the poor is ingenuous. Agee's "cruel radiance of what is" applies. Her imagination is empathetic but unsentimental: "So here comes the dog on the red bridge road," she wrote by way of explanation. "Was there a dog? Oh yes, there was a dog lay up there till he rotted, or weeds covered him or other animals drug off his bones. Or just direct. As a thing happened to me, or if not as altogether seen—as it moved in the mind. And I hope that it moves a little in someone else's mind."

Literary influences occasionally assert themselves in the poems in a dedication (e.g., there are poems to Robert Duncan, poems to John Gould Fletcher), or an internal reference, or with formal likenesses such as the pointedly imagistic poem "under holly". By and large, it is more fitting to declare, this is the legacy of a solitary reader and writer, who read because she loved it, and wrote because she had to. One could almost say writing was the key instrument of her humanity. Except for her family, she opted for the company of animals, domestic and wild, diurnal and nocturnal, whole and broken. Indoors is the place for illness or death or retreat from sudden weather. Outside is where the mind resides. Outside is home. When the young snake that lives under the house slithers out to get the sun, Besmilr arms herself first with her hoe; then with her pen as her husband greets him, "were you cold under the house he says / pretty thing." The Brighams' nomadism takes them to the deep north—to Nova Scotia and Alaska—but most of the time they head south by southwest — Arkansas, Mississippi, Texas, New Mexico, Mexico — and the writing strikes deepest in those regions. Brigham's writing is autochthonous, primally so. Thus, an American poet was "heaved from the earth," and occupied her numbered days shaping a rock-hard sensibility of extreme independence.

Meeting this unusual couple, in the driving heat of southern Arkansas, was an unforgettable occasion. Standing in her low-ceilinged living room, watching as the doors of her handmade cabinet opened onto dozens of carefully bound, mice-gnawed manuscripts will remain one of my most prized moments.

Quite simply, the gravitational field of the word has yet to relax its draw on us. How could anyone give up a space so implausible, so underrated, uncompromising, lost, deep and wild, downright weird, chosen, comforting, timeless and true, so near the aorta, so fitted to the brainpan, taut and tense, pressurized, so sheer and obscure, so glossal, igneous, voracious, horny and approximate to fulfillment, fulminating, probing, uninhibited, restive, rancorous and rad, so rank-and-file, saber-toothed, so irreducible as in stripped to its vitals, so mutinous, so sensational, sweet, and transfiguring?

While I sometimes prefer cornbread crumbled in buttermilk to sushi, I do not write from my lost life alone any more than I dictate every term by which I do write.

In my work I am led by my senses, but I understand practical matters. I am neither interested in preserving nor in exorcising the poetry of the hills. There are luminous albeit terrible facts I must simply transcribe. I the scribe. Others, transform. But on the same point, I submit you have to strike down your own mythology about yourself, your loves, your ravishing and atavistic homeland. I am interested in the vision beyond this confrontation. Boundaries of illumination between the created, the re-created, the newly gleaned, the as yet incomprehensible. Speaking for myself, this scribbling saves me from missing a minute of what would otherwise go unpondered, unqualified.

Writing is a risk and a trust. The best of it lies yonder. My linguistic skills expand on the horizon. So does the horizon. My goals are higher-minded than they once were. Once you could say, I had ambition. I never could write any old way. And like many from my generation, I desire the integrated life.

Uncommitted people do not hold my interest, period. Now that I have a little know-how, even readers, I am hungrier; I don't want to break bread with the word unless convinced I have something in the mix that bears kneading. And someone to finish off the wine with, who is listening. Who is intent. Who will read me the riot act when I shut up.

If I could have written some of the poems Yeats wrote in the late twenties and early thirties, or if I could have broken the ground Beckett broke, I might have a sense of my own solidity and prowess. I still feel I might turn an irrevocable corner. I want to keep pressing toward the outer edge of my own enterprise, and I want to apprehend my own burning core before the winds blow into their final snuff routine.

Poets are mostly voters and taxpayers, but the alienation of the poet is a common theme. Among poets there are also probably higher than average rates of clutch burnout, job turnover, rooting about, sleep apnea, noncompliance, nervous leg syndrome, depression, litigation, black clothing, and so forth, but this is where we live, or as Leonard Cohen put it, poetry is the opiate of the poets.

elation washed over our absence toward
everything in the increasing darkness.

The soft coloration of his longing in the indifferent
environment has never deserted me.
My husband saving the spermaceti to light
our eyestrings. My husband charting my obsessions
with characteristic cool. Singing sacerdotally
in the shower, my husband intoning every cleft in my skin.
Our syncopated breathing. My husband who flew often
at night as a child. Above the very ground
of our writing (even as power poles were falling
on volvos). My husband equally popular with women
of all ages. His nail parings, his running legs, his scriptoria.
O his ludic hard head. Who cut down
his own hair with a bone-handled knife. His rack
of gorgeous unworn ties. My husband touching
even the insular men; whenever fear bred
its mushrooms under rugs, a cleaning frenzy commenced.
Our bed irrigated with my blood. Watching me burn
from within; tendering his cross pen. O predominantly
white guilt. Whenever it rained

after h.l. hix

Every word I set down rightly involves overcoming an ingrained resistance to do otherwise.

The Ozarks are a fixture in my mindscape, but I did not stay local in every respect. I always think of Miles Davis, "People who don't change end up like folk musicians playing in museums, local as a motherfucker." I would not describe my attachment to home as ghostly, but long-distanced. My ear has been licked by so many other tongues.

The lacunae are there even if you are working against a wall of sound. There are gaps in everything. What is lineation if it is not about respecting the surrounding space. And the spaces in between.

It is fair to say I am interested in the formally anomalous poem, not the representatively formal poet, that is, when it comes to discrete poems. When it comes to extended poems, I am interested in a structure that is supportable, bottom up, as well as structure within the larger one, which will activate the whole.

Poetry and Parenting

are symbiotic — the relationship is close, protracted and not necessarily of benefit one to the other. They are different organisms, different species. There are certainly periods when they fill each other up, and there are just as certainly periods when they drain each other's cup. It is not my choice to forgo one for the other. I was asked by a poet, who had reluctantly chosen not to have children, what conditions I would require to become the best poet I could. And I had to allow, I had them, though I struggle for the opportunities to enter that clearing where I am alone and afraid and humbled and pregnant only with the anticipation of working without interruption. I had to allow that I require the distraction, that I require the attachment, and that unencumbered I merely dissipate; I come undone. I had to admit, I require the struggle though it brings me to my knees when I most long to be standing free.

Not Often Enough I Dream

that I write a consummate work, write while sleeping, on beautiful laid paper. The scripted pages float around the room, drift to the floor, onto covered furniture, and out an open casement. And sometimes when reading before sleeping, I fall into the same elated trance, having read something that so startles and pleases me it bears me aloft, and some part of me elopes with its secrets.

Once I had begun to read this vivid, intimate writing, there was no option but to read the entire, if only for the sake of provoking such effortless, formative dreaming.

Waking from this state is not a letdown, but a bit like leaving a matinee. There is an adjustment. Even when the experience is more akin to leaving a late show, one has to reenter the jostle, acknowledge a sudden hunger or thirst, remember where the car was parked and who drove. Yet the latent quality of the poetry or the prose is not what finally separates the reader from diurnity. No, the artful, conscious elements are those that break the reader free: the singularity of composition, the particular light given off by Ondaatje's vocabulary, and the persuasive nearness of attainment. As they say in Sri Lanka, "a well-told lie is worth a thousand facts"; the actual world does shear away. That quickly, that quietly. The reader is there for the duration, and leaves with reluctance.

When Keith Waldrop pointed out to me that Yeats began the edition he edited of *The Oxford Book of Modern Verse* with a paragraph by Walter Pater, which he (Yeats) liked, and so broke into lines and stanzas... I became once-and-for-all-time suspicious of line laws. If the Irish bard can open the quintessential English anthology of verse with an example of the precise, refined, and subtle prose of Pater... the only thing that seems clear to me about line, is that the melody of the language can be made visible if it falls under the right eye. Some of us arrive at our line early on and rarely write a poem that deviates from the original course. The lay of the line is shaped to the mind's eye in such a way that whatever needs saying on a given page in a given day can be said without being wrought into another pattern. The line satisfies a basic formal question, and opens everything else to further examination. If the line is soundly founded it can bear the corpus. For other writers the line that suits them best evolves. It demonstrates the quality of their workmanship over time. And for some the line is utterly mutable; its latency is in the poem being made. The poem discovers the line or the poem goes blind trying.

Readers have to be sought out and won to the light of the page, poem by poem, one by one by one. Readers rarely even arrive in pairs to ensure the continuation of the line.

If we are reaching the end point of art's authority, poetry seems to suspend itself at the serrated edge with its precious vial of significance, a final refusal against the venal surround. "The light is hyacinth," Julian Beck wrote, "poetry makes it clear."

Feel its heat.

Poetry's position is all but fixed in the poet's mind as the sole engagement (other than living itself) whose yield we consider worth the grief. "Poetry helps us to suffer more efficiently," the hieratic Jack Gilbert once told me.

If the incision of our words amounts to nothing but a feeling, a slow motion, it will still cut a better swath than the factory model, the corporate model, the penitentiary model, which by my lights are one and the same.

As in all callings, poetry secures a kind of ecstasis. There may be a wiser vantage, but we haven't discovered one yet. Perception leads to further perception. *Perceive. Perceive.* "See what the grass would see if it had eyes," writes Oppen.

This is the language we cannot usually hear for always speaking prose. It is more than passing strange, and it is sick of our daily casuistry.

We need to lower the veneration around the terms of communication and expression and aim to see better — and to see better we have to move at whatever pace we can tolerate in the direction of our blind spot, else learn to recognize its advance toward us — which is usually where we are most smugly and snugly ensconced. Best not expect any grand vista. I think this is linked to what Pema Chödrön calls the high-stakes practice of the bodhisattva vow. The Buddhist has "to stay right there with whatever comes through the door." And this is the knot and the nut of any art practice — which cannot be gained without hurtling into deep blindness in which even memory of sightedness is lost. When you have ventured toward your ignorance, that is where the whole comes ever so fleetly into view. As Pema Chödrön put it, gloriousness and wretchedness need each other.

Going home to the very town, the street and very house where we grew up is more often than not an overwhelmingly inarticulate experience. The onslaught of memories alone may not be manageable. However thin and colorless and tiny we remain in our original context, it is the one we are perpetually challenged and most equipped to render lucid.

One Carries an Exacting Memory
of Certain Reading Experiences,

like a scent, forever. It was snowing; I was at my brother's house
in Harrison, Arkansas. Reading on the couch while Warren
and his wife slept. An onionskin carbon of the manuscript in
two bulging brown folders on the end table. My clawless cross-
eyed cat adhered to my side, loudly idling. The picture window
faced the highway and the snow-covered field opposite. Inter-
mittent headlights appeared over the rise. The author stopped
by sometime in the night, on his way to or from somewhere,
and we walked up and down my brother's street in the snow.
The cat rode on his shoulder; I don't remember being capable
of saying much. I was embarrassed about everything: the
snow, the cat, the sleeping relatives, the dumb clothes I had
on. Most of all I wanted him to leave so I could read through
the night, uninterrupted by the forces already set in motion to
undo my ill-formed life. And he did not stay as he was on his
way to or from somewhere, and he knew I was reading his
poem, and he sensed I wanted him to go so I could be alone
with the poem to the end.

I took *The Battlefield Where the Moon Says I Love You*, on
impact, as a personal blow. Here was a poetry by someone
barely five months older than I, whose geography I knew,
whose lexicon I could grasp. He had put the intensity of his
mind to the task. I felt absolutely helpless to so much wildness
of heart, so much fury and hilarity, such language. My skin
burned, my insides hurt. I wanted to bury myself in the snow,
pull the pages down on top of me. I wanted the cat to curl
above me, mark the spot where we were buried, the poem and
I. Never was I to be this innocent again.

Going back in the summer is preferred to winter. When it's all leafed out. Grown over. Winter is bald. The hawks are seen as easily as they see us. We see the new houses on the denuded hills. The hawks see the denuded hills beyond the houses, where the newer ones will be. The hawks see the future too clearly. They are nowhere in it.

Going back is not the same as not going back. Going back is not the same as not going off to begin with. We leave to be who we will become. We go back to see who we are. We are no less than our struggle or that of our foes, even those we would make ciphers.

Who died there. Who is dying. Who forfeited a once-perfect breast. Whose once-lovely daughter fell asleep with a desolate cigarette. Whose body wears a bag to pee in. Who is 100% queer now. Who knew it all along. Whose youngest son drowned in their stupid bean-shaped pool. Who got born again. Who made a pile of money gypping people out of their savings. Who was a party switcher. Who came home from the city to help his widower father fend. Who is left. Who left.

Who shot himself to death in her paternal grandmother's bed. With a target pistol. Who ran in the room to straddle the body, pump the dead poet's chest. Who ran out the door. Who called the police.

Who opened their doors to the mourners. Who was wedded the same afternoon on Petit Jean mountain.

Who photographed the last blaze rose in the rented yard.

She remembers. She misremembers. She disremembers. Like everyone.

She goes back. She doesn't go down. There. Anymore. It is not poetry. It smells of mortality.

And here is the peeling rent house by the ravine. This is the ravine where she threw the telephone receiver to make herself stop calling and calling when one was there and the other was not.

This is where those who heard, who knew or thought they knew, or felt as if they had known, entered a separate landscape of pain and loneliness. Everyone came and stood apart like a boat in a field. Then came the young men in uniforms. One young woman in uniform. And the poet was covered, rather he was bagged, tagged, and taken away. Very little blood. Only powder burns. No more sound.

And those who came to hear, gradually, they came too, and sat on the stoop or stood in the garden more or less motionless. Photographs were taken of the last blaze rose. People who didn't like each other, who had never liked each other, felt a burning love. Backs were patted and the lady cat was stroked. Old stories got told. And they drank until they went to sleep wherever they folded over. And on the weekend came the musicians, out of the Delta and over the mountains in the beat-up bus.

The memory of it is very hard. It goes down. There. Geotropic. It would take a lengthy time to fell. It is not poetry. It is a scratched, repetitive record of loving. Unloving. Losing. Leaving.

Over here is the periphery. Whence you came. Can you describe it. In detail. What you remember is moving. Backward. You do not see the beginning. Words scumble the view. Here is the center of your enterprise. Your life. Almost miraculously, without a sound, it grew up around you protective and full. You abide in it. Volatile yet alive. Living. Loving. Loved. For the venation of one's own leaf. Into its plenary. Back there. Down. When. Is the ruinous forever. Yearning for perfection.

What *It* Is:

A rhomboid. Brilliant. Impenetrable. Which occurs in a pure state. ("As dense at the edge as at the centre.") A widely distributed nonradioactive element. Therefore, not to be confused with uranium. What is brought about by some of the most lustrous, least attractive wordsmiths. What cannot be fashioned into prose. Let that go as a very hard and a very cold definition.

Groping Along the Cold Walls of Silence:

Lately silence, as a high poetic value, has begun to seep into the marrow. Lately silence, as the formal element I have been missing, has shattered the noise. I yearn to surprise myself, quietly; to proceed from an increasingly less protected vantage.

This Much I Know:

Poetry will not go quietly. You would have to starve it out, and it can eat on very little. Hunger and love move the world, didn't Schiller say so.

Now:

Shut my eyes because the music is so loud. Shut my eyes so I
can recall what I just saw; so I can believe my eyes. I know this
world. I can reference it with shut eyes though the pictures
elect different references.

Landscape of big dogs, big melons, big-car longings and
dreams big as distant capitals.

This landscape, it teems with cast-iron frying pans, pitcher
beer, bait, guns, yard ornaments, buttons in a jar, rough-planed
walls, hair in brushes, riverworms, spirit-catching bottle trees,
drunken wrecks, dangerous infidelities, chemical plants, paper
mills, gourds, eels, mirrors chipping silver nitrate, floors
scored from moving furniture, etc., etc.

You can see this world with shut eyes like a zeppelin sailing
slowly across a screen or a flatiron taking off from the cooking
stove of its own accord.

This landscape, its inhabitants, hew to used things, worn
things, handmade things. Hew to objects loved by the maker
even if shot full of holes by the maker's hand via the maker's
eye: a riddled wooden deer made by hand to be a target, to be
shot full of holes. Follow the wooden curve of this world.

Follow the copper light of this eye. Most of the time Deborah
Luster photographs humankind. Formally, with the conven-
tional blackdrop; environmentally, where she finds them, work
or home, having a vision in their kitchen or picking okra in the
field line, doing time. A kid is pictured holding something wild
and alive he caught bare-handed. Some will stick their arms
into a submerged log; take home whatever takes hold. Hand-
fishing, in Louisiana.

The light's sultriness rubs off on the subfusc of flesh, foliage,
clothing. Tobacco-stained light. Sparerib theology. A ludic

tendency participates in all but the most sobering images. And in the most sobering images, one has to shut one's own eyes because the music is so loud. So one can believe one's own eyes.

Every portrait could be titled "you." The countenance directs the attention rather than the light source. Though here appears a glow. The light picks a face. There is no negligible face, no negligible place. Composition is maximally concentrated: a girl in baptism clothes holding a shell, an eyeful of folds within folds. She is backed by a profusion of canna lilies and clouds which amplifies her solitary glory. The lens is honed by emotional realism. Shoot for core temperature. The choices endless, and thus the decisions. Look for parallelism, not symmetry. Follow the curve, which she seems to prefer to sharp lines. And hard turns.

The faces are there like the comforting glow of a neighbor's television. But they are looking back at her, looking back at everyone out there, daring the viewer to see them now. How the viewer sees them is the viewer's business. Ideally, the interpretations spread.

If opposition is inevitable, her eye weighs against what would anneal or coarsen us. The viewer may glimpse the damage, but also its limits. These pictures commemorate our wild youth, our unyielding decrepitude, and eventual manumission. They bring their own references. The interior of experience. She shuts us up. The ears believe other people, goes the proverb; the eyes believe themselves.

Dearly Belated,

Le temps bouleverse tout / La renommée demeure
EPITAPH IN THE CEMETERY NEXT DOOR

I have heard, against a chorus of prophylactic concern, that
you are turning toward poetry. Young and confused. Drawn
there, too. I thought. Why me. I thought. Why not. Everything
else I could think to do seemed a homely duty or else an illu-
sion, worse, a lie, a betrayal, mired in money, meetings, or else
a mean substitute for a few reams of freedom.

On your way to your future — assuming it is yours to parlay
into a shape that may take you an age to discover and that
often includes moving in umpteen directions except forward
— you have been stayed by poetry. None of the generic terms of
art edify the way — style, voice, line, image, form, vision. My
presence is not needed to tell you that you must read practically
all, everybody, including, no, *especially* the ones who consider
it their prerogative and their due to vitiate even the open seat-
ing on the poetry exchange. Nor am I needed to suggest that
the process inevitably entails scratching among the artistic
remains of a host of byronically insane types; negotiating
among irreconcilable mental claims, and expelling enough
print to describe, embellish, evoke worlds without coming
anywhere in the vicinity of poetry. Much of your energy could
be paid out looking for a starting point. Hence, its perverted
fulfillment, beginning without end.

Is it from one's own deficiencies that this stuff issues, gets
translated into something implausibly worthy of setting down.
If this is your epilogue of love, if this is your license to soar,
your fugitive order for chaos, your lonely communal rite —
then where better to situate a modest empyrean.

Hope butted against hope. Your utmost, is it not, at worst, a self-constructed alternative to caving in. Is it not also greater than the sum of your assets. Even if not mensural.

Meanwhile. Nothing. Meanwhile. Something. Drawn there. Making choices where there were none to be made before. Not talking, walking, knocking, reacting, but taking up residence on this ancient stone wall where the only imperative is to be. Take a wide-angled pan of the fields. Not lift your arm to shield the light. Until the mind begins to fustigate in its casing. Then zoom. Plunge into the neglected garden below among the broken pots and nodding thistle.

And at the end of nearly everything, poetry, the old rose, by its very avowal, refuses to shut its merlot mouth. In the evening, I'll find you, dearly belated, troweling around a word. You won't need me to remind you, gods defecate here.

Approximately forever,

What Would Oppen Say,

What would Oppen say, he would say, "It is difficult now to speak of poetry —." And for twenty-five years he did not — from 1934–1958 — so abstemious was he in his relationship to his commitment to social change and so absolutist in his relationship to his art that he could not yield to programmatic ideals.

So, what does it mean *now* to sequester oneself for the single purpose of exploring the limits of one's language *in our time* when the accords of nations with respect to the fate of millions, with respect to the very viability of the world, are deemed anachronisms, that is, irrelevant by a handful of political hacks, war criminals, and profiteers who are more or less recognized as being in rightful control. *Now* that Max Weber's definition of *state* is the only fitting one: "a human community that (successfully) claims the monopoly of the legitimate use of physical force within a given territory." Period.

So, which is it *now, in our time, our only time,* an act of resignation, self-interest, or refusal to abdicate the language to the most powerful to write a poem that may or may not make the most minimal public appearance, and if it does, may or may not directly address the crises of our time.

The time has come to loot to hew and Eden, writes Marjorie Milligan, an obscure Providence poet. I take her line as a call to words. I submit that pressing the demands of the word forward is pertinent, urgent, a requirement even. The happiness that belongs to all of us has been stolen by the few, declared Rigoberta Menchú. I can't accept this outcome. I will not. Notwithstanding scale —

in our only time.

"Follow me," the voice, the long, longed-for voice stops
the writing hand. "I have your shoes." Except
for a rotating fan, movement at a minimum. The plan,
if one can call it a plan, is to be in what is known
to some as the perennial present; beginning
with a few sentences written in a kitchen while others
cling to their own images in twisted sheets of heat.
A napkin floats from a counter in lieu of a letter. Portals
of the back life part in silence: O verge
of song, O big eyelets of daylight. Leaving milk and bowl
on the table, leaving the house discalced. All this
mystery, mildly erotic. Even if one is terrified
of both death and the color red. Even if a message is sent
each of us in secrecy, no one can make it stay.
Notwithstanding scale — everything has its meaning,
every thing matters; no one a means every one an end

About the Author

C.D. Wright lives outside of Providence. She has published eleven collections of poetry, most recently *Steal Away: Selected and New Poems,* and *One Big Self: Prisoners of Louisiana* with photographer Deborah Luster. She is married to poet Forrest Gander. Both are on the faculty at Brown University. They have a son, Brecht. And a greyhound, Jackie.

The Chinese character for poetry is made up of two parts: "word" and "temple." It also serves as pressmark for Copper Canyon Press.

Founded in 1972, Copper Canyon Press remains dedicated to publishing poetry exclusively, from Nobel laureates to new and emerging authors. The Press thrives with the generous patronage of readers, writers, booksellers, librarians, teachers, students, and funders — everyone who shares the conviction that poetry invigorates the language and sharpens our appreciation of the world.

Major funding has been provided by:

The Paul G. Allen Family Foundation

Lannan Foundation

National Endowment for the Arts

The Starbucks Foundation

Washington State Arts Commission

THE **PAUL G. ALLEN**
FAMILY *foundation*

Lannan

NATIONAL
ENDOWMENT
FOR THE ARTS

STARBUCKS
FOUNDATION

WASHINGTON
STATE ARTS
COMMISSION

For information and catalogs:

COPPER CANYON PRESS
Post Office Box 271
Port Townsend, Washington 98368
360/385-4925
www.coppercanyonpress.org

Cooling Time is set in Kepler, a Multiple Master font designed by Robert Slimbach. Multiple Master fonts can be varied by weight, width, and set size to create variations of the face. Here, a medium width and an extended width indicate different classes of the text: prose, verse, and aphorisms. Book design and composition by Valerie Brewster, Scribe Typography. Printed on archival-quality Glatfelter Author's Text at McNaughton & Gunn, Inc. Special thanks to Douglas Humble for the use of his artwork throughout the book.